Table of Contents

Copyright © 2004 SingaporeMath.com Inc., Oregon

Using this Guide

This book is a *guide* for teachers using the Primary Mathematics. It is designed to help teachers understand the course material, to see how each section fits in with the curriculum as a whole, and to prepare the day's lesson. The course material is divided up into 80 sessions with one to three activities for each section. The second or third activities are optional games that can also be done during review sessions or in any later session. Sessions can be combined for one day's lesson by spending less time on class participation or discussion or not having as many problems for practice during class time.

This guide is designed to be used with both the U.S. edition and the third edition of *Primary Mathematics*. U.S. conventions and spellings are used in this guide, such as using commas for thousands and colons for time, and not using "and" in writing out whole numbers in words. However, any items specific to either edition, such as different answers, different page numbers, and different exercise numbers, are indicated with a superscript **US** or **3d**. There are some entire sessions on U.S. standard measurement that pertain only to the U.S. edition.

This guide includes some worksheets, which can be copied for single class use only.

Workbook exercises can be gone over in class or assigned as homework.

Suggested Material

Number discs
These are discs with 1, 10, 100, and 1000 written on them. Have some that can be displayed; you can write the numbers on transparent counters if you have an overhead projector. You can also simply draw circles on the board and label them. For student manipulatives, you can write the numbers on opaque counters. Each student or group should have 18 of each type.

Number cards
Various number cards for games or group activities, see materials list for each part. You can use index cards, but make sure that the number does not show through the card. Many activities will call for four sets of number cards 0-9 for each group. These can be made from playing cards by removing the face cards, making the Ace a 1, and whiting out the 1 and the symbols for the 10 to make them 0.

Hundreds board
This is a chart with squares in a 10 x 10 array numbered from 1 to 100. Have one that can be displayed and written on. You will also need to display a blank hundreds board, or a 10 x 10 array but without numbers in the squares. For students, you can use hundreds boards with spaces large enough to be covered up by counters, one for each student, or you can use paper hundreds boards.

Counters
Use the opaque round counters that will fit on a hundreds board, or cubes, or any suitable counter. They should be in 4-5 different colors.

Money
Use some dimes and pennies that can be displayed/stuck to the board. You can also simply draw them.

Number cubes
These are cubes that can be labeled with different numbers. You need 2 for each group of about 4 students.

Measuring tools

Meter sticks, measuring tapes in centimeters, yard sticks, rulers, various types of weighing scales, a balance, weights, measuring cups, and beakers or measuring cups marked in milliliters.

Fraction circles and bars

Use ones that can be displayed. You can also just draw them.

Demonstration clock and individual student clocks with geared hands

Hinged meter stick or other hinged strips

Squares and half-squares (triangles)

Connect-a-cubes or other linking cubes

These are cubes that can connect on all 6 sides.

Optional Resources

Vroot and Vroom CD-ROM

This CD-ROM contains learning activities and two games. Topics covered include material from both Primary Mathematics 3 and 4. The following chart correlates the different activities to the appropriate part of *Primary Mathematics 3B*.

Primary Mathematics 3B		*Vroot and Vroom Primary Three*
Anytime		Game 1
Unit 1 – Mental Math	Part 2 - Subtraction	Game 2, Mission 2

Unit 3 – Bar Graphs	Part 2 – More Word Problems	Graphs
		  Learn and Explore
		  Activity
		  Challenge

Unit 4 – Fractions	Part 1 – Fraction of a Whole	Fractions
		  Learn and Explore
		  Activity

	Part 4 – Comparing Fractions	Challenge
Unit 7 – Time	Part 2 – Other Units of Time	Game 2, Mission 4

Unit 8 – Geometry	Part 2 Right Angles	Angles
		  Learn and Explore
		  Activity
		  Challenge

Unit 9 – Area and Perimeter	Part 1 – Area	Area and Perimeter Learn and Explore 1

	Part 3 – Area of a Rectangle	Learn and Explore 2
		  Activity
		  Challenge 1
		  Challenge 2

Supplemental Workbooks

These optional workbooks provide a source of extra problems for more practice, tests, and class discussions. Some have interesting and thought-provoking non-routine problems for discussion.

Extra Practice for Primary Mathematics 3 (U.S. Edition)
This workbook has two to four page exercises covering topics from *Primary Mathematics* 3A and *Primary Mathematics 3B*. The level of difficulty and format of the problems is similar to that of the *Primary Mathematics*. Answers are in the back.

Primary Mathematics Challenging Word Problems 3 (U.S. Edition)
This workbook has word problems only. The problems are topically arranged, with the topics following the same sequence as *Primary Mathematics 3A* and *3B*; however, this book is more useful with *Primary Mathematics 3B* since only the first topic can be used before the last unit in *Primary Mathematics 3A*. Each topic starts with three worked examples, followed by practice problems and then challenge problems. Although the computation skills needed to solve the problems is at the same level as the corresponding *Primary Mathematics*, the problem solving techniques necessary in the challenge section are sometimes more advanced. For example, there are 3-step word problems, whereas *Primary Mathematics 3B* only has 2-step problems. It is a good source, though, of extra word problems that can be discussed in class or of enrichment problems for more capable students. Answers are in the back.

Primary Mathematics Intensive Practice 3B (U.S. Edition)
This supplemental workbook has one long exercise for each topic in Primary Mathematics. Each topical exercise has questions of varying levels of difficulty, but the difficulty level is usually higher than that in the Primary Mathematics textbook or workbook. Some of the word problems are quite challenging and require the students to extend their understanding of the concepts and develop problem solving abilities. There is also a section called "Take the Challenge!" with non-routine problems that can be used to further develop students' problem solving abilities. Answers are located in the back.

Unit 1 – Mental Calculation

Objectives
- Use mental strategies for adding and subtracting 2-digit numbers.
- Multiply tens and hundreds by a 1-digit number.
- Divide tens, hundreds, and thousands by a 1-digit number.

Suggested number of sessions: 8

	Objectives	Textbook	Workbook	Activities
Part 1 : Addition				**2 sessions**
1	▪ Review mental addition of ones or tens. ▪ Add numbers within 100 by adding first the tens and then the ones.	pp. 6-7	Ex. 1	1.1a 1.1b
2	▪ Add numbers within 100 by making tens.	p. 7	Ex. 2	1.1c 1.1d 1.1e
Part 2 : Subtraction				**2 sessions**
3	▪ Review mental subtraction of ones and tens. ▪ Subtract numbers within 100 by subtracting first the tens and then the ones.	pp. 8-9	Ex. 3, #1	1.2a
4	▪ Subtract numbers within 100 by subtracting from a ten.	p. 9	Ex. 3, #2	1.2b 1.2c
Part 3 : Multiplication				**1 session**
5	▪ Review multiplication of tens or hundreds by a 1-digit number.	p. 10	Ex. 4	1.3a 1.3b
Part 4 : Division				**1 session**
6	▪ Divide tens, hundreds, or thousands by a 1-digit number by removing and appending the correct number of 0's.	p. 11	Ex. 5	1.4a
Practice				**2 sessions**
7	▪ Review mental calculation. ▪ Solve word problems using mental calculation.	p. 12, Practice 1A p. 13, Practice 1B		1.5a
8				1.5b

Part 1: Addition **2 sessions**

Objectives

- Add numbers within 100 by adding tens and then ones.
- Add numbers within 100 by making tens or a hundred.

Materials

- Displayable number discs for 1, 10, and 100.
- Number discs for students.
- Number cards 10, 20, 30, 40, 50, 60, 70, 80, and 90; one set for each group.
- 4 sets of number cards 0-9 for each group.
- Hundreds board, one for each group.
- Counters

Homework

- Workbook Exercise 1
- Workbook Exercise 2

Notes

In *Primary Mathematics 2A* and *Primary Mathematics 3A*, students learned to add using a vertical format and the formal algorithm in which the ones were added first, 10 ones renamed as a ten, and then the tens added. The student still needs to practice the formal algorithm and can use it when needed.

However, using mental calculation strategies increases number sense. Some of the mental math strategies learned in earlier levels of *Primary Mathematics* will be reviewed in this and the next lesson. Although these strategies will be discussed in the activities, allow your students to use any strategy in mental calculation, including strategies not yet introduced.

Mental math strategies learned in earlier levels of *Primary Mathematics* and new ones introduced here include the following. (Number bonds are shown here to illustrate these strategies, but students should not be required to draw these number bonds.)

➢ Add 1, 2, or 3 by counting on.
$\quad$ 59 + 2 = 61; count on 60, 61.

➢ Add two 1-digit numbers whose sum is greater than 10 by making a 10. (This strategy is useful for students who know the addition and subtraction facts through 10, but have trouble memorizing the addition and subtraction facts through 20.)

$\quad$ 7 + 5 = 12

$$7 + 5 = 10 + 2 = 12$$
$$3 \quad 2$$

$$7 + 5 = 10 + 2 = 12$$
$$2 \quad 5$$

➢ Add tens to 2 digit numbers by adding the tens.

$\quad$ 48 + 20 = 68

$$48 + 20 = 68$$
$$8 \quad 40$$

- ➢ Add a 1-digit number to a 2-digit number by adding the ones together.

  $47 + 2 = 49$

  $47 + 2 = 40 + 9 = 49$
  $\overset{\diagup\,\diagdown}{40\ \ 7}$

- ➢ Add a 1-digit number to a 2-digit number where adding the ones results in a number greater than 10 by
  - o making a 10
  - o or by using basic addition facts.

  $68 + 5 = 73$

  $68 + 5 = 70 + 3$
  $\overset{\diagup\diagdown}{\,2\ \ 3}$
  $68 + 5 = 60 + 13 = 73$
  $\overset{\diagup\diagdown}{60\ \ 8}$

- ➢ Add a 2-digit number to a 2-digit number by adding the tens and then the ones, using the strategies already learned for adding tens and 1-digit numbers.

  $48 + 25 = 73$

  $\qquad +20 \qquad +5$
  $48 \longrightarrow 68 \longrightarrow 73$

- ➢ Add a 2-digit number to a 2-digit number by making a ten. (This strategy is new here.))

  $48 + 25 = 50 + 23 = 73$

  $48 + 25 = 50 + 23 = 73$
  $\qquad\quad\overset{\diagup\diagdown}{2\ \ 23}$

- ➢ Add a 2-digit number to a 2-digit number by adding the next ten and then subtract an appropriate number of ones. (This strategy is new here.)

  $48 + 25 = 25 + 50 - 2 = 75 - 2 = 73$

- ➢ Add a number close to 100 by making 100.

  $57 + 98 = 155$

  $57 + 98 = 55 + 100 = 155$
  $\overset{\diagup\diagdown}{55\ \ 2}$

- ➢ Add a number close to 100 by first adding 100 and then subtracting the difference.

  $57 + 98 = 57 + 100 - 2 = 157 - 2 = 155$

If your students have used *Primary Mathematics* previously and have been using mental math strategies all along, spend less time on the review in the first activity.

There are mental math sheets at the end of each section in this unit. Students can work on them independently, or for homework, or you can put one problem at a time on the board and have students take turns answering them. You can have a "sprint" where students see how many they can answer in a certain amount of time. Mental math practice can continue into later units. Students should also periodically practice the standard addition algorithm for numbers within 10,000 (e.g. $5862 + 4109 = ?$) — you can give students one or two such problems a day or at intervals, perhaps at the beginning of class, along with a few mental math problems. Students should be able to determine whether to use mental strategies or the standard algorithm in solving a problem.

Activity 1.1a   **Mental math strategies for addition**

1. Review mental addition of a 1-digit number.
   - Draw a 10 by 2 array of squares on the board. Color in 7 squares in one row.
     - Write the expression 7 + 3 and ask a student to solve it. 7 + 3 = 10.
     - Color in another 3 squares with a different color to show all ten squares in a row colored.

7 + 3 = 10

   - Draw another 10 by 2 array and color in 7 squares.
     - Write the expression 7 + 5 and ask a student to solve it. The student may recall the addition fact 7 + 5 = 12.
     - Color in 3 more squares and remind the students that 7 and 3 more make a ten. So far we have added 3. Ask how much more we have to add to add 5 in all?   2 more. Color in 2 more squares in the next row. Draw the number bond showing 5 split up into two numbers, the one that makes a 10 with 7 and what is left.
     - Repeat by first coloring in 5 squares to show that we can also make a 10 with the 5.

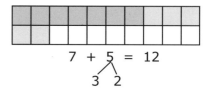

7 + 5 = 12
      3 2

7 + 5 = 12
  2 5

8 + 7 = 15
    2 5

   - Repeat with a few other examples.
   - Draw a 10 x 5 array and color 37 squares.
     - Ask a student how many squares are colored.
     - Write the expression 37 + 5 and ask a student to solve it.
     - Color 3 more squares with a different color and ask how many squares are colored so far, then color another 2 squares. Draw the number bond to show this. We can add by making 40 with 37 using part of the second number (5).
     - Rewrite the expression. Tell your students we are going to talk about another way to add 37 + 5.
       - We are first going to find the tens of the answer. Ask them if they can tell just from looking ahead to the next place, the ones, whether adding the second number will create another ten. It will. What will be the total number of tens?   4 tens. Write down a 4 for the tens of the answer.
       - Now we are going to find the ones.
         - Since 7 + 5 = 12, and we already added in the extra ten, all we need to do now is write down the ones.
         - Or, we can also find the ones by thinking of the number left over from the 5 after making a ten with 37. Write down the ones.

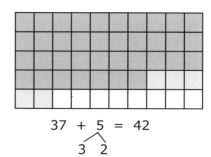

37 + 5 = 42
      3 2

37 + 5 = **4_**

37 + 5 = 4**2**

   - Repeat with a few other examples. Allow the students to use any strategy. A student might, for example, add 48 + 9 by first adding 10 and then subtracting 1.

2. Review the strategy of mentally adding tens to a 2-digit number. Use number discs to illustrate.
    - Write the expression 37 + 80.
        o Display 3 tens and 7 ones. Display another 8 tens. Remind your students that 36 is 3 tens and 8 ones.
        o Write the number bond. Move the 8 tens over by the 3 tens and ask your student to add the tens.
            ▪ We can add 3 tens and 8 tens using the same strategies for adding 3 ones and 8 ones. Ask for the sum of 3 and 8 (3 + 8 = 11).
              3 tens + 8 tens = 11 tens.
        o Replace ten of the 10-discs with a 100-disc.
        o Write 11 tens after the equation, with a line indicating the ones place. We have 11 tens so far.
        o The ones will just be the 7 from 37. Write 7 down for the ones.
    - Repeat with a few other examples. Include some where there is no renaming of the tens.

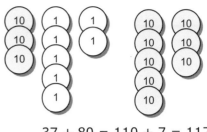

$37 + 80 = 110 + 7 = 117$

$7 \quad 30$

$37 + 80 = \mathbf{11\_}$

$37 + 80 = 11\mathbf{7}$

3. Discuss mental addition of 2-digit numbers by first adding the tens and then the ones. Use number discs to illustrate.
    - Write 36 + 45 = ? on the board and display two corresponding sets of number discs.
    - Move the tens from the second number over by those of the first number. Ask a student to add the tens. Write the partial answer for 36 + 40 using an arrow diagram as shown here.
    - Move the ones over with the rest of the discs. Ask a student to add the ones to the 76. Use an arrow diagram to show 76 + 5.
    - Write the answer to the original expression.
    - Students should not be required to write the partial sum unless a problem asks for it. They are learning mental math, not just another way of writing out a problem. They can keep 76 in mind and mentally add 5 to it.

$36 + 45 = ?$

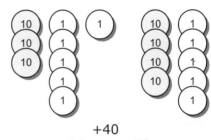

$$36 \xrightarrow{+40} 76$$

$$36 \xrightarrow{+40} 76 \xrightarrow{+5} 81$$

$36 + 45 = 81$

4. Discuss textbook, **p 6**

5. Discuss **tasks 1-3, p. 7** in the textbook.
    - Call on students to supply the answers.
    - Have the student explain the strategy he or she used for tasks 2 and 3.

6. Discuss a strategy in which we add by finding each digit from right to left. You can use tasks 3.(g), (h), or (i). For example, write the expression 55 + 26.
    - Find the tens first. Look ahead to the ones – will adding the ones increase the tens? Yes, so add the tens and increase the sum by 1. Write 8 for the tens.
    - Find the ones: 5 + 6 = 11, so the ones is 1. Write 1 for the ones.

$55 + 26 = \mathbf{8\_}$

$36 + 45 = 8\mathbf{1}$

Workbook Exercise 1

Activity 1.1b   **Mental math with 3-digit numbers**

Some students may be able to extend these strategies to 3 digit numbers. You may want to discuss mental addition of 3-digit numbers using this optional activity. This activity can also be done at a later time during a review for enrichment. Use Mental Math practice 2 for practice problems.

1. Adding ones to a 3-digit number.
   - Write $356 + 8$. Discuss ways to add these numbers. Illustrate with number discs.
     - Lead the students to see that adding the ones will not change the hundreds, the hundreds stay the same. Write 3 for the hundreds.
     - Add $56 + 8$ using the same strategies already discussed. Write down the tens and then the ones.

     - Ask students for an example where adding the ones will change the hundreds. For example, $297 + 8$.
       - Work through the problem with the students. In this case, we could write 3 down for the hundreds, and then add 97 and 8 to get 105, write 0 for tens and 5 for ones. $297 + 8 = 305$.
       - Methods for adding numbers close to a hundred were given in *Primary Mathematics 2B*, and will be reviewed in the next activity. A student might remember these strategies and suggest adding 300 to 8 and subtracting 3.
       - We could also count up 10 and back 2.

$$356 + 8 =$$

$$356 + 8$$
$$\diagup\ \diagdown$$
$$300\quad 56$$

$$356 + 8 = \mathbf{3}\_\_$$

$$356 + 8 = 3\mathbf{6}\_$$

$$356 + 8 = 36\mathbf{4}$$

$$297 + 8 = 305$$

2. Adding tens to a 3-digit number.
   - Write the expression $237 + 80$. Discuss ways to add these. Illustrate with number discs.
     - Since we are adding tens, we can ignore the ones for now, and think of 237 as 230 and 7.
     - Since 230 is 23 tens, we can add 8 tens using the same strategies for adding $23 + 8$. $23 + 8 = 31$. 23 tens + 8 tens = 31 tens.
     - Once we find the tens, we can write that down and then write down the ones.
   - Repeat with some other examples. Allow students to use whatever strategy they want. A student might, for example, add 237 and 80 by adding 100 and subtracting 20.

$$237 + 80$$
$$\diagup\ \diagdown$$
$$7\quad 230$$

$$237 + 80 = \mathbf{3}\_\_$$

$$237 + 80 = 3\mathbf{1}\_$$

$$237 + 80 = 31\mathbf{7}$$

   - You can let the students try some problems involving adding a 2-digit number to a 3-digit number, if your students are doing well with mental calculations.

Activity 1.1c　　　　　　　　**More mental math strategies for addition**

1. Refer to **task 4, p. 7** in the textbook.
   - Tell your students this is another strategy for adding numbers mentally.
   - You can illustrate the process with number discs. Display or draw 5 tens and 8 ones, and next to them 1 ten and 6 ones and write the equation $58 + 16$ underneath.
     - Point to the 8 ones and ask how many more are needed to make a ten.
     - Move 2 of the ones over from the 16 to make a ten with the 8 ones from 58. Replace those ones with a 10-disc and ask how many tens there are now on the left. There are 6 tens. By taking away 2 from 16, there are now 14 ones, so $58 + 16$ becomes $60 + 14$.

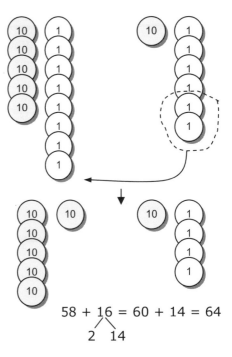

$$58 + \underset{2 \quad 14}{16} = 60 + 14 = 64$$

   - You can also illustrate the process with a blank 100 chart. This provides some additional visual reinforcement of the process. Use a new example, such as $47 + 24$. Color in squares on both sides to represent the two numbers that are to be added together. Point to the side representing the larger number and ask how much more is needed to make the next ten? If you take that from the other number, only tens and one set of ones is left.

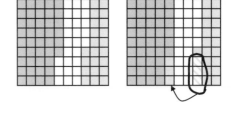

$$47 + \underset{3 \quad 21}{24} = 50 + 21 = 71$$

2. Discuss a strategy for adding two numbers when one is close to a ten by adding a ten and taking away the excess.
   - Point out to your students that in $58 + 16$, 58 is close to 60. What would happen if we added 60 to 16? We get 76, but we have added 2 too many. So we can then remove the 2 extra to get 74. You can illustrate the process with number discs.
   - Ask your students when they might want to use this strategy. They would use it when adding a number close to a ten.
   - Provide additional examples.

$$\begin{aligned} 16 + 58 &= 16 + 60 - 2 \\ &= 76 - 2 \\ &= 74 \end{aligned}$$

$$\begin{aligned} 47 + 67 &= 47 + 70 - 3 \\ &= 117 - 3 \\ &= 114 \end{aligned}$$

3. Review addition of 95 to 98 by adding 100 and then taking away the excess. This was already covered in *Primary Mathematics 2B*, and used in the money unit in *Primary Mathematics 3A*. See the example at the right.
   - You can also review adding 3-digit numbers ending in 95 to 98.

$$58 + 98 = 58 + 100 - 2$$
$$= 158 - 2$$
$$= 156$$

$$58 + 298 = 58 + 300 - 2$$
$$= 358 - 2$$
$$= 356$$

4. Have students do **task 5, p. 7** in the textbook. They can also try doing tasks **3(g) – 3(i), p. 7** using the strategy of making tens or adding tens and subtracting the excess.

Workbook Exercise 2

Activity 1.1d   **Add two 2-digit numbers**
Game

In this game, students will be using 4 randomly drawn digits to form two 2-digit numbers with the lowest possible sum. In order to get the lowest sum, the tens digits for both numbers will have to be the two cards with the smallest number. It will not matter what digit each ten gets as its ones. For example, if the numbers drawn are 2, 4, 9, and 8, the 2 and 4 must be used for the tens to get the lowest sum. The two possible combinations are 29 + 48 or 28 + 49, both of which give the same sum.

Material for each group of about 4 students:
- Four sets of number cards 1-9.

Procedure:
- Shuffle cards and place face-down in the middle.
- Each player draws four cards. They arrange the cards into two 2-digit numbers that will give the lowest sum.
- They then compare their sums. The player with the lowest sum gets a point.
- Play continues until all cards have been turned over. The player with the most points wins.
- Variation: Players could also write down their sums and keep a running total, using mental math to find the sum from the cards, and use either mental math or the addition algorithm to find a running total. The player with the lowest total at the end of 3 rounds wins.

Activity 1.1e   **Add two 2-digit numbers**
Game

In this game, students will be forming 4 randomly drawn digits into two 2-digit numbers whose sum is less than or equal to 100. If one of the numbers drawn is 0, they can make a 1-digit number if the 0 is used as a ten.

There are only a limited number of possible ways to arrange the cards. For example, if the four numbers are 2, 8, 6, and 3, we can find all the possible combinations by first making a 4-digit number and then splitting it into two 2-digit numbers. Any of the four digits can go in the first place, any of the remaining 3 digits in the second place (giving 4 x 3 = 12 possibilities), any of the remaining 2 digits in the third place (giving 4 x 3 x 2 = 24 possibilities) and the remaining number has to go in the last place. So there are potentially 24 possible arrangements for the 4 numbers. Since the first and second pair of numbers can be interchanged after we split the 4-digit number into two 2-digit numbers, this over-counts half the possibilities, reducing the number of possibilities to 12. In this example, the first digit can't be 8, because none of the other numbers can be used as the first digit of the second number to get a sum less than or equal to 100. We end up with 6 possibilities, but since half of them give same sum as the other half, there are only 3 possible sums.

$$28 + 63 = 91$$
$$28 + 36 = 64$$
$$26 + 38 = 64$$
$$23 + 68 = 91$$
$$62 + 38 = 100$$
$$68 + 32 = 100$$

At this level, do not spend time showing the students a systematic way to find all the possible sums. They will discover that 8 can't be used as one of the tens, which eliminates half the possibilities, and that some pairs give the same sum.

If one of the digits is 0, it can be used in the tens place to make a 1-digit number. For example, if 3, 4, 8 and 0 are drawn, one possible set of numbers is 34 and 8.

Material for each group:
• Four sets of number cards 0-9.
• Hundreds board.
• Counters, a different color for each player.

Procedure:
• Shuffle cards and place face-down in the center.
• All students draw 4 cards. They then arrange the cards into two 2-digit numbers. The sum must be no greater than 100. A 0 can be used as a ten to make a 1-digit number.
• When the student has formed the number and found the sum, he or she places a counter on the hundreds board to cover up an uncovered number corresponding to the answer. If it is already covered, the digits should be rearranged to make different numbers with a different sum, if possible. If not, they can exchange one of their cards with a new card and try again.
• Play continues until a student gets 3 counters in a row, or until students have covered up a specified number of squares on the hundreds board, such as 20 of them.
• Students can cooperate in determining how to arrange the cards so that the sum is not a number that is already covered up.

This game can be done as a class activity, with groups working together to form a suitable set of numbers, and marking a hundreds board at the front of the room.

Mental Math Practice 1

1. $14 + 3 =$ _____

2. $17 + 9 =$ _____

3. $89 + 3 =$ _____

4. $46 + 5 =$ _____

5. $32 + 8 =$ _____

6. $45 + 2 =$ _____

7. $23 + 60 =$ _____

8. $45 + 50 =$ _____

9. $28 + 6 =$ _____

10. $32 + 4 =$ _____

11. $56 + 9 =$ _____

12. $49 + 70 =$ _____

13. $42 + 8 =$ _____

14. $28 + 60 =$ _____

15. $92 + 50 =$ _____

16. $8 + 39 =$ _____

17. $59 + 40 =$ _____

18. $80 + 46 =$ _____

19. $58 + 3 =$ _____

20. $5 + 53 =$ _____

21. $72 + 70 =$ _____

22. $5 + 32 =$ _____

23. $6 + 57 =$ _____

24. $40 + 38 =$ _____

25. $8 + 13 =$ _____

26. $4 + 85 =$ _____

27. $4 + 47 =$ _____

28. $86 + 30 =$ _____

29. $70 + 77 =$ _____

30. $91 + 30 =$ _____

Mental Math Practice 2

1. $148 + 3 = $ _____

2. $172 + 9 = $ _____

3. $899 + 3 = $ _____

4. $426 + 5 = $ _____

5. $328 + 8 = $ _____

6. $451 + 2 = $ _____

7. $234 + 60 = $ _____

8. $451 + 50 = $ _____

9. $528 + 6 = $ _____

10. $322 + 4 = $ _____

11. $506 + 9 = $ _____

12. $490 + 70 = $ _____

13. $422 + 8 = $ _____

14. $286 + 60 = $ _____

15. $902 + 50 = $ _____

16. $80 + 391 = $ _____

17. $509 + 40 = $ _____

18. $80 + 446 = $ _____

19. $548 + 3 = $ _____

20. $5 + 537 = $ _____

21. $726 + 70 = $ _____

22. $5 + 327 = $ _____

23. $6 + 573 = $ _____

24. $40 + 382 = $ _____

25. $8 + 134 = $ _____

26. $4 + 853 = $ _____

27. $4 + 427 = $ _____

28. $862 + 30 = $ _____

29. $70 + 767 = $ _____

30. $691 + 30 = $ _____

Mental Math Practice 3

1. $51 + 50 =$ _____
2. $53 + 48 =$ _____
3. $55 + 46 =$ _____
4. $58 + 43 =$ _____
5. $82 + 44 =$ _____
6. $43 + 57 =$ _____
7. $86 + 14 =$ _____
8. $66 + 24 =$ _____
9. $80 + 42 =$ _____
10. $95 + 13 =$ _____
11. $52 + 73 =$ _____
12. $48 + 34 =$ _____
13. $32 + 78 =$ _____
14. $67 + 43 =$ _____
15. $91 + 49 =$ _____
16. $95 + 35 =$ _____
17. $29 + 98 =$ _____
18. $59 + 62 =$ _____
19. $24 + 87 =$ _____
20. $36 + 77 =$ _____
21. $42 + 99 =$ _____
22. $28 + 44 =$ _____
23. $92 + 95 =$ _____
24. $42 + 97 =$ _____
25. $82 + 71 =$ _____
26. $48 + 65 =$ _____
27. $34 + 55 =$ _____
28. $68 + 84 =$ _____
29. $99 + 44 =$ _____
30. $77 + 82 =$ _____

Part 2: Subtraction   **2 sessions**

Objectives

- Subtract numbers within 100 by subtracting tens and then ones.
- Subtract numbers within 100 by subtracting from the nearest ten.

Materials

- Displayable money (dimes and pennies).
- Displayable number discs for 1, 10, and 100.
- 4 sets of number cards 1-9 for each group.

Homework

- Workbook Exercise 3

Notes

In *Primary Mathematics 2A* and *Primary Mathematics 3A*, students learned to subtract using a vertical format and the formal algorithm. The student still needs to practice the formal algorithm and can use it when needed.

Mental math strategies learned in earlier levels of *Primary Mathematics* and new ones introduced here include the following.

➢ Subtract 1, 2, or 3 by counting back.
    $51 - 2 = 49$; count back 50, 49.
    $302 - 3 = 299$; count back 301, 300, 299

➢ Subtract tens from a 2-digit numbers by subtracting the tens.

    $48 - 20 = 28$

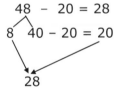

➢ Subtract a 1-digit number from a 2-digit number when there are enough ones by subtracting the ones.

    $47 - 2 = 45$

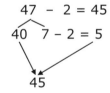

➢ Subtract a 1-digit number from a 2-digit number when there are not enough ones by

    o   subtracting from a 10.

    o   or by using basic subtraction facts.

    $65 - 8 = 57$

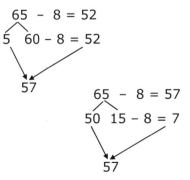

➤ Subtract a 2-digit number from a 2-digit number by subtracting the tens and then the ones, using the strategies already learned for subtracting tens and 1-digit numbers.

$$75 - 38 = 37 \qquad 75 \xrightarrow{-30} 45 \xrightarrow{-8} 37$$

➤ Subtract a 2-digit number from a 2-digit number by subtracting from the nearest ten. (This strategy is new here.)

$$75 - 38 = 37$$

$$75 - 38$$
$$35 \quad 40 - 38 = 2$$
$$37$$

➤ Subtract a 2-digit number from a 2-digit number by subtracting the next ten and then adding back in an appropriate number of ones. (This strategy is new here.)

$$75 - 38 = 75 - 40 + 2 = 35 + 2 = 37$$

➤ Subtract a number close to 100 by subtracting 100 and then adding back the difference.

$$457 - 98 = 457 - 100 + 2 = 357 + 2 = 359$$

If your students have not used earlier levels of *Primary Mathematics*, spend some time with the concept of subtracting from the ten. Although your students may be comfortable with subtracting by recalling the subtraction facts, and able to use that in mental calculations, the idea of subtracting from the next higher place value has applications in the sections on subtracting measurements in compound units.

There are some mental math pages at the end of this section.

Provide periodic practice with the standard algorithm for subtraction for numbers under 10,000, as learned in *Primary Mathematics 3B*, as you move into other units. Students should be able to discern when to use the algorithm and when to use mental math strategies.

Activity 1.2a   **Mental math strategies for subtraction**

1. Review subtraction of a 1-digit number by subtracting from a ten. You can use dimes and pennies. Use ones that you can display, or draw them like number discs on the board.

   - Display a dime and 3 pennies. Write the equations and/or number bonds as you elicit answers in the following discussion:
     - *How much money is this?* (13 cents)
     - *We want to buy something that costs 7 cents. What would we give the cashier, the dime or the pennies? Since there are not enough pennies, we would give the dime.*

       $13 - 7 = 3 + 3 = 6$

       $3 \quad 10$
     - *What change would we get?* (3 cents).
     - Replace the dime with 3 pennies.
     - *How much money do we now have?* (6 cents)
     - *To get the amount we now have, we had to add the change to the pennies we started with.*
   - Display 4 dimes and 3 pennies.
     - *How much money is this*? (43 cents)
     - *We want to buy something that costs 7 cents. What would we give the cashier?* (One of the dimes) How much change would we get? (3 cents)
     - Replace a dime with 3 pennies.
     - *How much money do we now have?* (36)

       $43 \quad - 7 = 33 + 3 = 36$

       $33 \quad 10$
     - *We have one less dime, and the number of pennies is the sum of the change from a dime and the pennies we started out with.*
   - Give students some other problems for practice.

2. Review subtraction of a ten from a 2-digit number.
   - Display 4 dimes and 8 pennies. Write the equation 48 – 20. We have 48 cents and want to buy something that costs 20 cents. We can pay using two dimes. We are left with 20 cents.

     $48 - 20 = 28$

     $8 \quad 40$

3. Refer students to the textbook, **p. 8**.
   - Discuss the first equation. You can illustrate the process on the board using number discs.

     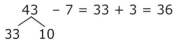

     $$63 \xrightarrow{\;-20\;} 43 \xrightarrow{\;-8\;} 35$$
   - Discuss **task 1**. Illustrate with number discs.
   - Discuss the last step in (c). Ask students to explain how they did the intermediate step 43 - 8.

   - Discuss 1.(c) again showing how we can omit writing down the intermediate step by looking ahead.

     $63 - 28 = \mathbf{3}\_$
     - Will subtracting the ones decrease the tens? Yes, so subtract the tens, and then write one less ten.

       $63 - 28 = 3\mathbf{5}$
     - Then find the ones.

4. Discuss **tasks 2-4, p. 9** in the textbook. Have students supply the answers.

Workbook Exercise 3, problem 1

Activity 1.2b   **More mental math strategies for subtraction**

1. Refer to **p. 9, task 5** in the textbook. Illustrate this process with dimes and pennies. Write a number bond as you discuss the process. Your discussion could go something like this, starting with 9 dimes:
   - *I have 9 dimes and want to buy something that costs 18 cents. What do I give the cashier?* (2 dimes)
     - *What is the change?* (2 pennies) Replace 2 dimes with 2 pennies.
     - *How much money do you have now?* (7 dimes and 2 pennies, or 72 cents).

$$90 - 18 = 72$$
$$70 \quad 20$$

   - Show how we can also do this subtraction by counting on.
     - *If we count up from 18 to the next ten, how much is that?* (2).
     - *What is the next ten?* (20)
     - *How many from the next ten to 90?* (70)
     - *We have counted up a total of 2 and 70, or 72.*

$$18 \xrightarrow{+2} 20 \xrightarrow{+70} 90$$

   - Show the strategy of subtracting tens and adding back the necessary ones. Since 18 is almost 20, we can subtract 20 and add back the 2.
     - *What would we get if we took away 20 instead of 18?.* (70) Take away 2 dimes.
     - *How much too much have we subtracted compared to 90 – 18?* (2).
     - *So we need to add 2 more back in to make up for subtracting 2 to many.* Add back 2 pennies.

$$90 \xrightarrow{-20} 70 \xrightarrow{+2} 72$$

2. Have students supply the answers for **p. 9, task 6** in the textbook.

3. Review subtracting a number close to 100, such as 98, by subtracting 100 and adding back in the difference.

$$192 - 98 = 192 - 100 + 2$$
$$= 92 + 2$$
$$= 94$$

4. Discuss how we could use the idea of subtracting from a ten, or subtracting the next ten, to do a problem such as 92 – 18, where we are subtracting from tens and ones, rather than just tens. We can use the same strategies we used for 90 – 18, but we have two more ones.

$$92 - 18 = 72 + 2 = 74$$
$$72 \quad 20$$

$$92 - 18 = 92 - 20 + 2$$
$$= 72 + 2 = 74$$

Workbook Exercise 3, problem 2

Activity 1.2c   **Subtract from tens**
Game

In this game, students will be forming 3 randomly drawn digits into a ten and a 2-digit number and mentally subtracting the 2-digit number from the ten (e.g. 80 – 32).

Material:
- Four sets of number cards 1-9 for each group of about four students.

Procedure:
- Shuffle cards.
- The dealer deals 3 cards to each player.
- The highest card of the three is a ten. The player forms a 2-digit number out of the other two cards and subtracts it from the 10. For example, a 5, 8, and 2 are turned over. The 8 is used as 80. The player uses the 5 and 2 to make 52 and subtract it from 80 to get 28.
- The player with the greatest difference gets a point. Play continues until all cards have been turned over.
- The player with the most points wins.

Mental Math Practice 4

1. $49 - 5 =$ _____

2. $96 - 3 =$ _____

3. $42 - 8 =$ _____

4. $33 - 7 =$ _____

5. $25 - 6 =$ _____

6. $81 - 9 =$ _____

7. $73 - 6 =$ _____

8. $54 - 8 =$ _____

9. $37 - 2 =$ _____

10. $60 - 20 =$ _____

11. $63 - 20 =$ _____

12. $82 - 30 =$ _____

13. $94 - 30 =$ _____

14. $85 - 50 =$ _____

15. $79 - 44 =$ _____

16. $162 - 90 =$ _____

17. $243 - 80 =$ _____

18. $184 - 60 =$ _____

19. $32 - 7 =$ _____

20. $23 - 4 =$ _____

21. $54 - 7 =$ _____

22. $72 - 7 =$ _____

23. $55 - 20 =$ _____

24. $477 - 90 =$ _____

25. $153 - 8 =$ _____

26. $294 - 2 =$ _____

27. $259 - 5 =$ _____

28. $743 - 5 =$ _____

29. $566 - 7 =$ _____

30. $136 - 9 =$ _____

Mental Math Practice 5

1. $98 - 29 =$ _____

2. $84 - 45 =$ _____

3. $73 - 39 =$ _____

4. $82 - 18 =$ _____

5. $23 - 17 =$ _____

6. $66 - 29 =$ _____

7. $53 - 35 =$ _____

8. $60 - 46 =$ _____

9. $42 - 38 =$ _____

10. $55 - 29 =$ _____

11. $60 - 44 =$ _____

12. $92 - 39 =$ _____

13. $22 - 15 =$ _____

14. $85 - 56 =$ _____

15. $32 - 16 =$ _____

16. $80 - 68 =$ _____

17. $30 - 14 =$ _____

18. $74 - 77 =$ _____

19. $60 - 28 =$ _____

20. $43 - 6 =$ _____

21. $90 - 4 =$ _____

22. $27 - 19 =$ _____

23. $70 - 57 =$ _____

24. $295 - 78 =$ _____

25. $148 - 35 =$ _____

26. $145 - 97 =$ _____

27. $134 - 98 =$ _____

28. $157 - 99 =$ _____

29. $120 - 95 =$ _____

30. $399 - 196 =$ _____

Part 3: Multiplication	**1 session**

Objectives

• Review multiplication of tens or hundreds by a 1-digit number.

Materials

• Displayable number discs for 1, 10, and 100.
• 4 sets of number cards 1-9 for each group.
• Number cubes labeled with "1", "10", "100" twice, one for each group.

Homework

• Workbook Exercise 4

Notes

In *Primary Mathematics 3A* students learned how to multiply tens and hundreds by a one digit number. This is reviewed here.

This skill will be used in later levels of *Primary Mathematics* to estimate the answer to a multiplication problem. For example: 3826 x 4 ≈ 4000 x 4.

The focus in this section is to have the students append the correct number of zeros.

Students learned to multiply numbers within 1000 by a 1-digit number using the multiplication algorithm in *Primary Mathematics 3A*. Give your students problems such as 356 x 8 = ? periodically during the semester, particularly during reviews.

Activity 1.3a   **Multiply tens or hundreds**

1. Review multiplication of tens and hundreds by a 1-digit number. Use number discs to illustrate.
   - Display or draw 2 groups of 3 ones.
     - Ask students how many there would be if there were 2 groups of 3 ones.
     - Write the equation, using "ones", and then using the standard equation.
   - Display 2 groups of 3 tens.
     - Ask students how many there would be if there were 2 groups of 3 tens.
     - Write the equation using "3 tens" and then using "30". Underline the 0's to emphasize that we are multiplying tens.
   - Display 2 groups of 3 hundreds.
     - Ask students how many there would be if there were 2 groups of 3 hundreds.
     - Write the equation using "3 hundreds" and then using "300". Underline the 0's to emphasize that we are multiplying hundreds.
   - Point out that we can multiply the non-zero digits together, and then add the correct number of zeros onto the product.
   - Write some other similar problems and ask students to find the products.
   - Include problems where there is a 0 from the multiplication, such as 4 x 5. 4 tens x 5 = 20 tens, so there are two 0's after the 2 in the product for 40 x 5, even though 40 had only one 0 after the 4.
   - Make sure your students understand that they multiply the non-zero digits together, write the product down, and then add the appropriate number of 0's. The final product may include more 0's than the original number.

2. Discuss textbook, **p. 10**. Have students do **tasks 1-2**.

Workbook Exercise 4

3 ones x 2 = 6 ones
3 x 2 = 6

3 tens x 2 = 6 tens
3<u>0</u> x 2 = 6<u>0</u>

3 hundreds x 2 = 6 hundreds
3<u>00</u> x 2 = 6<u>00</u>

4   x 5 = 20

4<u>0</u> x 5 = 20<u>0</u>

4<u>00</u> x 5 = 20<u>00</u>

Activity 1.3b   **Multiply ones, tens, or hundreds by a 1-digit number**
Game

Material for each group:
- Four sets of number cards 1-9.
- A number cube labeled with "1", "10", or "100" twice.

Procedure:
- Shuffle cards and place face down in the middle.
- Players take turns drawing 2 cards and rolling the dice.
- They select one of the cards to make into a one, ten, or hundred according to the number rolled on the dice. They then multiply that by the number on the other card and write down the product. For example, A player draws 4 and 8, and rolls a "10". He or she chooses the higher number (8) to make into tens (80) and then writes 80 x 4 = 320.
- After 3 rounds each player adds their three products together (using the addition algorithm or mental math strategies). The player with the highest sum wins.

Mental Math Practice 6

1. $50 \times 5 =$ _____

2. $60 \times 9 =$ _____

3. $500 \times 7 =$ _____

4. $700 \times 8 =$ _____

5. $80 \times 6 =$ _____

6. $9 \times 90 =$ _____

7. $600 \times 6 =$ _____

8. $3 \times 600 =$ _____

9. $40 \times 8 =$ _____

10. $9 \times 500 =$ _____

11. $300 \times 7 =$ _____

12. $3 \times 30 =$ _____

13. $300 \times 9 =$ _____

14. $2 \times 500 =$ _____

15. $30 \times 4 =$ _____

16. $800 \times 8 =$ _____

17. $5 \times 60 =$ _____

18. $800 \times 3 =$ _____

19. $8 \times 9 =$ _____

20. $7 \times 70 =$ _____

21. $80 \times 5 =$ _____

22. $600 \times 7 =$ _____

23. $9 \times 70 =$ _____

24. $400 \times 6 =$ _____

25. $900 \times 2 =$ _____

26. $70 \times 4 =$ _____

27. $4 \times 90 =$ _____

28. $400 \times 4 =$ _____

29. $4 \times 200 =$ _____

30. $20 \times 8 =$ _____

Part 4: Division	1 session

Objectives

- Divide tens or hundreds by a 1-digit number.

Materials

- Displayable number discs for 1, 10, and 100.
- 4 sets of number cards 0-9 for each group.
- Number cubes labeled with "1", "10", "100" twice, one for each group.

Homework

- Workbook Exercise 4

Notes

In *Primary Mathematics 3A* students learned how to divide numbers within 1000 by a one digit number, with or without remainders. Here, they will learn to divide tens, hundreds, or thousands mentally when the resulting quotient is a whole number.

This skill will be used in later levels of *Primary Mathematics* to estimate the answer to division problems. They will be replacing the dividend and possibly the divisor by close numbers with a simple quotient. For example, $4359 \div 6$ can be estimated by $4200 \div 6$, and $1359 \div 58$ can be estimated by $4200 \div 60$.

The focus in this section is to have the students append the correct number of zeros.

Students should continue to practice the division algorithm. Give your students problems such as $356 \div 8 = ?$ periodically during the semester, particularly during reviews.

Activity 1.4a   **Divide tens, hundreds, or thousands by a 1-digit number**

1. Use number discs to illustrate division of 8, 80, and 800 by 2.
   - Display or draw 8 ones.
     - Ask your students for the number of discs that would go into each group if you divided these by 2. Separate them into 2 groups.
     - Write the equation using "ones" and then using the standard equation.

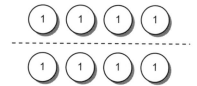

8 ones ÷ 2 = 4 ones
8   ÷ 2 = 4

   - Display 8 tens.
     - Ask your students for the number of tens that would go into each group if you divided these by 2. Separate them into 2 groups.
     - Write the equation using "tens" and then using the standard equation.
     - Underline the zeros to show that there are the same number of zeros in the number being divided and in the quotient.

8 tens ÷ 2 = 4 tens
80   ÷ 2 = 40

   - Display 8 hundreds
     - Ask your students for the number of hundreds that would go into each group if you divided these by 2. Separate them into 2 groups.
     - Write the equation using "hundreds" and then using the standard equation.
     - Underline the zeros to show that there are the same number in the number being divided and the quotient.

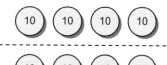

8 hundreds ÷ 2 = 4 hundreds
800   ÷ 2 = 400

   - Lead the students to see that in each of these problems, we are simply dividing 8 by 2 and then adding on the correct number of 0's

   - Write the expressions 40 ÷ 8 and 400 ÷ 8. Have students supply the answer.
     - Point out that 40 ÷ 8 is 5, so 40 tens ÷ 8 is 5 tens. The quotient does not always have the same number of 0's as the number we are dividing.

40 ÷ 8 = 5

400 ÷ 8 = 50

   - Summarize the process and provide other examples.
     - We can cover up the 0's on the first number (either with a finger or in our minds), one at a time, from the right. With zero or zeros covered, this number has to be larger than the number we are dividing by. Divide this number, and append the same number of 0's we took off.

3000 ÷ 5 = 600

2. Discuss textbook, **p. 11.** Have students do **tasks 1-2.**

3. Students learned to divide with remainders in *Primary Mathematics 3A*. They should be able to recognize when we cannot divide tens, hundreds, or thousands by a 1-digit number to get a quotient without a remainder.

- Write $20 \div 3$. Tell student that if we cover up the first 0, the 2 that is left is smaller than 3, so we can't cover up the 0. Ask for the quotient. We divide 18 by 3 and get a remainder of 2
- Write $200 \div 3$. If we cover up the last 0 for 200, we do not get a number that can be divided by 3. So for this problem we will have a remainder.
- You can step through the division problem as a review.

$20 \div 3 = 2 \text{ R2}$

$200 \div 3 = 66 \text{ R2}$

$$\begin{array}{r} 66 \\ 3\overline{)200} \\ \underline{18} \\ 20 \\ \underline{18} \\ 2 \end{array}$$

Workbook Exercise 5

Mental Math Practice 7

1. $720 \div 9 =$ _____

2. $120 \div 6 =$ _____

3. $6300 \div 9 =$ _____

4. $5600 \div 8 =$ _____

5. $420 \div 7 =$ _____

6. $8100 \div 9 =$ _____

7. $4800 \div 8 =$ _____

8. $240 \div 6 =$ _____

9. $450 \div 9 =$ _____

10. $3600 \div 6 =$ _____

11. $280 \div 4 =$ _____

12. $900 \div 3 =$ _____

13. $56 \div 8 =$ _____

14. $250 \div 5 =$ _____

15. $1000 \div 5 =$ _____

16. $2400 \div 3 =$ _____

17. $490 \div 7 =$ _____

18. $270 \div 9 =$ _____

19. $3200 \div 8 =$ _____

20. $180 \div 2 =$ _____

21. $200 \div 5 =$ _____

22. $5400 \div 9 =$ _____

23. $1800 \div 3 =$ _____

24. $400 \div 8 =$ _____

25. $3500 \div 7 =$ _____

26. $360 \div 4 =$ _____

27. $3000 \div 6 =$ _____

28. $210 \div 7 =$ _____

29. $1500 \div 5 =$ _____

30. $160 \div 4 =$ _____

Practice	**2 sessions**

Objectives

- Practice mental math calculations.
- Solve word problems.

Materials

- Blank hundreds board or 10 x 10 grid.

Notes

Mental strategies for subtracting from 100 were taught in *Primary Mathematics 2B*. In Unit 2 of *Primary Mathematics 3B*, students will be adding and subtracting in compound units. For the metric system they can do much of it using mental strategies involving subtracting from 100 or 1000. You may want to review these strategies now, using activity 1.5a. Otherwise, you can save the activity for use in Unit 2.

Use the two practices on pp. 12-13 as a source of problems to practice and review the material from this unit.

As you discuss the word problems, review the use of the part-whole and comparison models for addition, subtraction, multiplication, and division. These were introduced in *Primary Mathematics 3A*. If you are not familiar with them, please refer to the *Primary Mathematics 3A* Teacher's Guide for an explanation. A few of the problems are modeled for you in activity 1.5b

As part of this practice, do any of the games activities already suggested for this unit, and/or use the mental math practice pages. You can also review the addition, subtraction, multiplication, and division algorithms for numbers within 10,000. No all problems students will encounter need to be solved mentally!

You can assign parts of the practices for homework. If you do, you may want to copy them on a separate sheet and give students room to work out the answers.

Activity 1.5a   **Subtract from 100 or 1000**

1. Review subtraction from 100.
   - Write a problem, such as 100 – 34, on the board and ask your students for suggestions on how to solve it mentally.
   - Discuss the two methods that were taught in *Primary Mathematics 3*. You can use a 10x10 grid to illustrate both methods. Color in the correct number of squares.

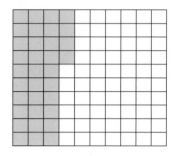

$$100 - 34 = ?$$

$$34 \xrightarrow{+6} 40 \xrightarrow{+60} 100$$

or

$$34 \xrightarrow{+60} 94 \xrightarrow{+6} 100$$

   - Method 1: Count on to find the answer.
     - Count on to the next ten, then by tens to 100.
     - Or, count on by tens to 9_, then by ones to 100.

   - Method 2: make 9 with the tens and 10 with the ones.
     - 100 is the same as 9 tens and 10 ones. On the hundreds board, three tens (the whole column) are colored, and 6 columns are not. If we already have 3 tens, we need 6 more tens (3 tens + 6 tens = 9 tens).
     - For the last column, 4 ones are colored, and 6 are not. We need 6 more ones (4 + 6 = 10)
     - By adding 6 tens and 6 ones, we now have 9 tens and 10 ones, or 100. 34 + 66 = 100, or 100 – 24 = 66.

$$100 \begin{array}{l} \nearrow 90 - 30 = 60 \searrow \\ \searrow 10 - 4 \ = 6 \nearrow \end{array} 66$$

$$\begin{array}{r} 90 + 10 \\ - \ 30 + 4 \\ \hline 60 + 6 \end{array}$$

$$100 - 34 = 66$$

   - Provide some additional problems.

2. Discuss subtraction of a 2-digit number from hundreds.
   - 400 – 34 = ?
     - We can take 34 away from one of the hundreds, so we write down one less hundred, (3), find 100 – 34, and write the answer down for tens and ones.
   - Provide some additional problems.

$$400 - 34 = ?$$

$$\begin{array}{c} 400 - 34 = ? \\ 300 \quad 100 - 34 = 66 \\ \searrow \quad \swarrow \\ 366 \end{array}$$

$$400 - 34 = 366$$

3. Discuss mental subtraction from 1000.
   - 1000 – 300 = ?
     - We can think of this problem as 10 hundreds – 3 hundreds = 7 hundreds and use 10 – 3 = 7 to find the answer.

$$1000 - 300 = 700$$

   - 1000 – 340 = ?
     - We can think of this problem as 100 tens – 34 tens. From 100 – 34 = 66, we can find 1000 – 340 = 660.
     - Or, we can think of 1000 as 900 + 10 tens. We then subtract 300 and 4 tens.

$$1000 - 340 = 660$$

$$\begin{array}{r} 900 + 10 \text{ tens} \\ - 300 + 4 \text{ tens} \\ \hline 600 + 6 \text{ tens} \end{array}$$

- $1000 - 345 = ?$
  - We can think of 1000 as 9 hundreds, 9 tens, and 10 ones.
  - For the hundreds, find the difference between 3 and 9. 9 hundreds – 3 hundreds = 6 hundreds
  - For the tens, find the difference between 4 and 9. 9 tens – 4 tens = 5 tens
  - For the ones, find the difference between 5 and 10. 10 ones – 5 ones = 5 ones

$1000 - 345 = 655$

$$1000 \to \begin{array}{l} 900 - 300 = 600 \\ 90 - 40 = 50 \\ 10 - 5 = 5 \end{array} \to 655$$

- $1000 - 34 = ?$
  - Think of 34 as 034, and 1000 as 9 hundreds, 10 tens, and 10 ones.
  - The hundreds is 9 hundreds – 0 hundreds = 9 hundreds.
  - The tens is 9 tens – 3 tens = 6 tens
  - The ones is 10 ones – 4 ones = 6 ones.

$1000 - 34 = 966$

$$1000 \to \begin{array}{l} 900 - 000 = 900 \\ 90 - 30 = 60 \\ 10 - 4 = 6 \end{array} \to 966$$

- $1000 - 7 = ?$
  - Think of 7 as 004, and 1000 as 9 hundreds, 10 tens, and 10 ones.
  - The hundreds is 0 hundreds – 0 hundreds = 9 hundreds.
  - The tens is 9 tens – 0 tens = 9 tens
  - The ones is 10 ones – 7 ones = 3 ones.

$1000 - 7 = 993$

$$1000 \to \begin{array}{l} 900 - 000 = 900 \\ 90 - 00 = 90 \\ 10 - 7 = 3 \end{array} \to 993$$

- $4000 - 345 = ?$
  - Split 4000 into 3000 and 1000. Write the 3 for the thousands place in the answer, and then solve 1000 – 345 as above.

$$4000 - 345 = ?$$
$$3000 \quad 1000$$

4. Provide some other examples for practice. You can use the Mental Math Practice 9 problems.

$4000 - 345 = 3655$

Activity 1.5b   **Word Problems**

Have students work individually or in groups on the problems on **pp. 12-13, Practices 1A or 1B** in the textbook, and then have some share their solutions.

Possible diagrams for some of the problems are shown here.

Practice 1A, p. 12

10.(a) 84 – 29 = 55

   55 is 29 less than 84.

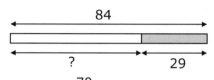

13. 1 unit = 70
     4 units = 70 x 4 = 280.

     He sold **280** USmuffins 3dbuns on Sunday.

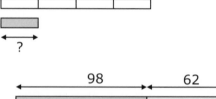

Practice 1B, p. 13

6.   4 units = 200
     1 unit = 200 ÷ 4 = 50

     The shop sold 50 chocolate cakes.

10. (a) 98 + 62 = 160

     He bought **160** pens.

     (b) 160 ÷ 8 = 20

     There were **20** pens in each box.

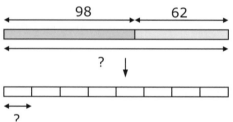

Note that problems 9 and 10 of Practice 1B require the student to realize that the (a) part must be solved before there is enough information to solve the (b) part.

Mental Math Practice 8

1. $30 \times 8 =$ _____

2. $49 + 71 =$ _____

3. $32 + 47 =$ _____

4. $60 - 28 =$ _____

5. $123 - 7 =$ _____

6. $49 + 17 =$ _____

7. $420 \div 7 =$ _____

8. $82 - 39 =$ _____

9. $300 \div 5 =$ _____

10. $74 - 6 =$ _____

11. $100 - 33 =$ _____

12. $2 \times 4000 =$ _____

13. $90 - 62 =$ _____

14. $57 - 32 =$ _____

15. $1111 - 9 =$ _____

16. $45 + 97 =$ _____

17. $89 - 34 =$ _____

18. $49 + 5 =$ _____

19. $67 + 56 =$ _____

20. $6 \times 500 =$ _____

21. $7 \times 70 =$ _____

22. $3500 \div 5 =$ _____

23. $30 \times 9 =$ _____

24. $4000 \div 8 =$ _____

25. $8100 - 9 =$ _____

26. $42 + 8 =$ _____

27. $8100 - 90 =$ _____

28. $182 - 95 =$ _____

29. $999 - 62 =$ _____

30. $8100 \div 9 =$ _____

Mental Math Practice 9

1. $100 - 4 =$ _____

2. $100 - 30 =$ _____

3. $100 - 25 =$ _____

4. $100 - 47 =$ _____

5. $100 - 21 =$ _____

6. $100 - 62 =$ _____

7. $100 - 8 =$ _____

8. $100 - 44 =$ _____

9. $100 - 75 =$ _____

10. $100 - 91 =$ _____

11. $100 - 19 =$ _____

12. $800 - 50 =$ _____

13. $700 - 80 =$ _____

14. $400 - 63 =$ _____

15. $300 - 77 =$ _____

16. $1000 - 980 =$ _____

17. $1000 - 210 =$ _____

18. $1000 - 730 =$ _____

19. $1000 - 30 =$ _____

20. $1000 - 50 =$ _____

21. $1000 - 4 =$ _____

22. $1000 - 6 =$ _____

23. $1000 - 871 =$ _____

24. $1000 - 532 =$ _____

25. $1000 - 88 =$ _____

26. $1000 - 31 =$ _____

27. $9000 - 340 =$ _____

28. $5000 - 680 =$ _____

29. $3000 - 120 =$ _____

30. $6000 - 742 =$ _____

Unit 2 – Length

Objectives
- Review meters and centimeters as units of length.
- Recognize kilometers and miles as units of length.
- Convert between meters and centimeters.
- Convert between kilometers and meters.
- Add or subtract meters and centimeters in compound units.
- Add or subtract kilometers and meters in compound units.
- [US]Review yards, feet, and inches as units of length.
- [US]Convert between yards and feet and between feet and inches.
- [US]Add or subtract yards and feet in compound units.
- [US]Add or subtract feet and inches in compound units.
- [US]Add or subtract miles.

Suggested number of sessions: 13

	Objectives	Textbook	Workbook	Activities
Part 1 : Meters and Centimeters				**4 sessions**
9	• Review meters and centimeters as units of length. • Find the number of centimeters in a meter.	pp. 14-15		2.1a
10	• Convert a measurement in meters and centimeters to centimeters and vice versa. • Make 1 m with centimeters.	pp. 15-16, 18 Practice 2A, # 1-3	Ex. 6	2.1b
11	• Add meters and centimeters in compound units.	pp. 17-18 Practice 2A, #4(a)-4(d), 6	Ex. 7, #1-2	2.1c
12	• Subtract meters and centimeters in compound units.	pp. 17-18 Practice 2A, #4(e)-4(h), 5	Ex. 7, #3-4	2.1d
Part 2 : Kilometers				**3 sessions**
13	• Understand the kilometer as a unit of measurement. • Convert a measurement in kilometers and meters to meters and vice versa. • Convert a measurement in meters to kilometers to meters. • Make 1 kilometer with meters.	pp. 19-21, 23 Practice 2B, #1-3	[US]Ex. 8 [3d]Ex. 8-10	2.2a
14	• Add kilometers and meters in compound units.	pp. 22-23 Practice 2B, #4.(a)-4.(d)	[US]Ex. 9, #1-2 [3d]Ex.11,#1-2	2.2b
15	• Subtract kilometers and meters in compound units.	p. 22-23 Practice 2B, #4(e)-5	[US]Ex. 9, #3-4 [3d]Ex.11,#3-4	2.2c

	Objectives	Textbook	Workbook	Activities
[US]**Part 3 : Yards, Feet and Inches**				**4 sessions**
16	▪ Review yards, feet, and inches as units of length. ▪ Measure in yards, feet, and inches. ▪ Convert between yards and feet. ▪ Subtract feet from 1 yard.	[US]pp. 24-25, 28 Practice 2C, #1, 3, 5.(a)–5.(c)	[US]Ex. 10, #1-2	2.3a
17	▪ Convert between feet and inches. ▪ Memorize multiplication and division facts for 12. ▪ Subtract inches from 1 foot.	[US]pp. 25, 28 Practice 2C, # 2, 4, 5.(c)-5.(e)	[US]Ex. 10, #3-5	2.3b
18	▪ Add or subtract yards and feet in compound units.	[US]pp. 28, Practice 2C, #6		2.3c
19	▪ Add or subtract feet and inches in compound units.	[US]pp. 26, 28 Practice 2C, #7	[US]Ex. 11, #1-4	2.3d
[US]**Part 4 : Miles**				**1 session**
20	▪ Recognize the mile as a unit of length. ▪ Add or subtract miles.	[US]p. 27	[US]Ex. 11, #5-6	2.4a
[US]**Practice**				**1 session**
21	▪ Practice.	[US]p. 28, Practice 2C		2.5a

Part 1: Meters and Centimeters	4 sessions

Objectives

- Review meter and centimeter as units of length.
- Estimate and measure lengths in meters and centimeters.
- Convert between meters and centimeters.
- Add or subtract meters and centimeters in compound units.

Materials

- Meter sticks, measuring tapes
- Rulers for each student with centimeter markings.
- String or ribbon.

Homework

- Workbook Exercise 6
- Workbook Exercise 7

Notes

In *Primary Mathematics 2A* students learned about the meter and centimeter as units of length. They estimated and measured lengths to the nearest meter or centimeter. This is reviewed in this section. Students should have plenty of practical experience measuring lengths and should have some idea of the length of their arms, hands, or feet or width of their palms or fingers to help them estimate length in other objects. For example, if the width of a finger is 1 cm, they can visualize (in their minds) the number of fingers-wide an object is. This helps them to estimate its width in centimeters.

The conversion of measurements will be learned for the first time here. Students will learn that 1 m = 100 cm. Remind students that they have already done conversion with money in *Primary Mathematics 2B* with 1 dollar = 100 cents. Similarly, they will learn to convert a measurement in meters and centimeters to centimeters, and to convert a measurement in centimeters which is greater than 100 cm to meters and centimeters.

Students will also learn to add and subtract in compound units. Although addition and subtraction of compound units can be performed by converting the meters into the centimeters and then adding or subtracting with the formal algorithm, encourage students to use mental strategies. Skills and strategies that can be used when adding and subtracting compound units in the metric system include renaming, mental addition and subtraction of 2-digit and 3-digit numbers, and making 10 (subtracting centimeters from meters) or 1000 (subtracting meters from a kilometer).

Activity 2.1a   **Estimate and measure lengths in meters and centimeters**

1. Review meters.
   - Refer to textbook, **p. 14**. Use several meter sticks. Have your students carry out activities similar to those described on this page.
   - In class, avoid the word "approximate". Use the term "about" instead, such as in, "The table-top is *about* 2 meters long."

2. Review centimeters.
   - Have students look at their rulers and find the centimeters.
   - Have them estimate and measure some lengths to the nearest centimeter. They can pair up to use two rulers to find longer lengths.
   - Some suggestions:
     o Find the width of your thumb.
     o Find the distance straight across from the tip of your thumb to the tip of your index finger when your thumb is spread out from the rest of your hand.
     o Find the distance from your elbow to the tip of your fingers.
     o Find something that is about 10 cm long.
     o How close to 8 cm can you cut a piece of string without measuring first?
     o Use a ruler to draw a line 3 cm long. Draw a line 10 cm long.
     o Without a ruler, draw a line 5 cm long. Then measure to see how close you came.

3. Have students measure in meters and centimeters.
   - Have students look at the meter stick or measuring tape and find the number of centimeters in a meter.
   - Have them measure objects longer than a meter to the nearest centimeter using several meter sticks or measuring tape, and record the lengths in meters and centimeters. They can measure their heights using a meter stick and some rulers, or mark their height on a wall with masking tape and then measuring the distance from the floor to the tape.

$$1 \text{ m} = 100 \text{ cm}$$

Activity 2.1b   **Convert between meters and centimeters**

1. Convert from meters and centimeters to centimeters.
   - Discuss **task 1, p. 15** in the textbook.
     o Remind students that 1 m = 100 cm. Write 1 m = 100 cm on the board.
     o Illustrate the problem with a diagram.
   - Discuss **task 2, p. 15**.
     o Also ask students for the number of centimeters in other multiples of a meter. Write the equations.
   - **Task 3, p. 15**
     o Students can do this task in pairs or in small groups. One student walks 5 steps and the others measure the distance.

$$1 \text{ m} = 100 \text{ cm}$$

1 m 25 cm = 125 cm

100 cm   25 cm

1 m = 100 cm
4 m = 4 x 100 cm   = 400 cm
7 m = 7 x 100 cm   = 700 cm
9 m = 9 x 100 cm   = 900 cm
30 m = 30 x 100 cm = 3000 cm

- Discuss a conversion problem where the number of centimeters is less than 10, such as 6 m 5 cm.
  - o Ask students why the following answers are **wrong**:
    - 6 m 5 cm = 65 cm
    - 6 m 5 cm = 650 cm

6 m 5 cm = 605 cm

600 cm   5 cm

- Have students do **tasks 4-5, p. 16**.
- Use **Practice 2A, problem 1, p. 18** for more practice.

2. Convert centimeters to meters and centimeters.
   - Have students convert centimeters in multiples of 100 to meters.

200 cm = 2 m
400 cm = 4 m
700 cm = 7 m

- **Task 6, p. 16**
  Show a number bond splitting 395 cm into 300 cm and 95 cm and have students convert 300 cm to meters.

395 cm = 3 m 95 cm

300 cm   95 cm
3 m

- Have students do **tasks 7-8, p. 16**.

- For more practice, have students do **Practice 2A, problem 2, p. 18**.

3. Have students use mental math strategies for "making 100" to "make 1 meter".
   - Write: 45 cm + _____ = 1 m
     - o Ask students how many more centimeters are needed to make 1 m.
     - o They should use the mental math strategies for making 100, since 1 m = 100 cm.

45 cm + _____ = 1 m
45 cm + 55 cm = 1 m

- Discuss some other problems. They can be written as a subtraction, such as 1 m – 30 cm or 1 m – 5 cm.

1 m – 30 cm = _____
1 m – 5 cm = _____

- Write a problem such as 2 m – 1 m 45 cm
  - o Lead students to see that 1 m 45 cm is less than 2 m, so they can find the answer by "making 100" with 45 cm.

2 m – 1 m 45 cm = 55 cm

- Discuss solutions to the problems in **Practice 2A, problem 3, p. 18**. You can have students work on these problems independently first, and then call on some to explain how they solved them. Encourage students to use mental strategies in which they subtract from 100. For (d) you can draw a number bond. For (f), note that we can simply subtract the centimeters.

Workbook Exercise 6

Activity 2.1c   **Add meters and centimeters in compound units**

1. Discuss some addition problems where only centimeters are added to meters and centimeters, and the sum of the centimeters is less than 100.
   - We can simply add the centimeters together.

   $$2 \text{ m } 60 \text{ cm} + 2 \text{ cm} = 2 \text{ m } 62 \text{ cm}$$
   $$2 \text{ m } 60 \text{ cm} + 25 \text{ cm} = 2 \text{ m } 85 \text{ cm}$$
   $$2 \text{ m } 65 \text{ cm} + 28 \text{ cm} = 2 \text{ m } 93 \text{ cm}$$

2. Discuss some problems where centimeters are added and the sum of the centimeters is greater than 100. 100 cm will have to be renamed as 1 m, such as 2 m 60 cm + 75 cm
   - We can add the centimeters together, and then convert that sum into meters and centimeters, giving one more meter.
   - Or, we can "make 100 with either the 75 cm or the 60 cm. There will be one more meter, and the remainder after making 100 is the number of centimeters
     (Later, as students become more comfortable with compound units, they may omit writing down the intermediate step. Looking ahead, they can see when the adding of centimeters sums to over 100 cm, and write down one more meter before finding the centimeters.)
   - Or, we can use the addition algorithm. We can think of 2 m 60 cm as 260 cm, add 75 cm, and convert the answer back to m and cm.

   $$2 \text{ m } 60 \text{ cm} + 75 \text{ cm}$$

   $$2 \text{ m } 60 \text{ cm} \xrightarrow{+\ 75 \text{ cm}} 2 \text{ m } 135 \text{ cm} = 3 \text{ m } 35 \text{ cm}$$

   $$2 \text{ m } 60 \text{ cm} + 75 \text{ cm} = 2 \text{ m } 35 \text{ cm} + 100 \text{ cm}$$
   $$= 3 \text{ m } 35 \text{ cm}$$
   (35 cm, 25 cm)

   $$2 \text{ m } 60 \text{ cm} + 75 \text{ cm} = 2 \text{ m } 100 \text{ cm} + 35 \text{ cm}$$
   $$= 3 \text{ m } 35 \text{ cm}$$
   (40 cm, 35 cm)

   ```
   2 m 60 cm  ⟶ 260 cm
   +     75 cm   +  75 cm
   3 m 35 cm  ⟵ 335 cm
   ```

3. Discuss some problems where both centimeters and meters are added, and the sum of the centimeters is less than 100 (no renaming).
   - Add the meters first, then the centimeters.
   - This can be recorded as
     $$2 \text{ m } 65 \text{ cm} + 3 \text{ m } 20 \text{ cm}$$
     $$= 5 \text{ m } 65 \text{ cm} + 20 \text{ cm}$$
     $$= 5 \text{ m } 85 \text{ cm}$$

   $$2 \text{ m } 65 \text{ cm} + 3 \text{ m } 20 \text{ cm}$$

   $$2 \text{ m } 65 \text{ cm} \xrightarrow{+\ 3 \text{ m}} 5 \text{ m } 65 \text{ cm} \xrightarrow{+\ 20 \text{ cm}} 5 \text{ m } 85 \text{ cm}$$

4. Discuss some problems where both centimeters and meters are added, and the sum of the centimeters is more than 100 (requiring renaming).
   - Add the meters first, then the centimeters.
   - Add the centimeters using the same strategies used in item 2.
   - This can be recorded as
     $$2 \text{ m } 65 \text{ cm} + 3 \text{ m } 40 \text{ cm}$$
     $$= 5 \text{ m } 65 \text{ cm} + 40 \text{ cm}$$
     $$= 6 \text{ m } 5 \text{ cm}$$

   $$2 \text{ m } 65 \text{ cm} + 3 \text{ m } 40 \text{ cm}$$
   2 m   65 cm   3 m   40 cm

   $$2 \text{ m } 65 \text{ cm} \xrightarrow{+\ 3 \text{ m}} 5 \text{ m } 65 \text{ cm} \xrightarrow{+\ 40 \text{ cm}} 6 \text{ m } 5 \text{ cm}$$

(Students can look ahead and see if the adding of centimeters will come out to more than 100 cm, but be slow to let students skip the intermediate steps, since otherwise some student may begin making errors.)

- Students can also write the problem vertically, convert meters to centimeters, use the addition algorithm, and then convert back.

$$\begin{array}{r} \overset{1}{2}\ 6\ 5 \quad cm \\ +\ 3\ 4\ 0 \quad cm \\ \hline 6\ 0\ 5 \quad cm = 6\ m\ 5\ cm \end{array}$$

5. Discuss **task 9.(a), p. 17** in the textbook.

6. Have students do **practice 2A, problems 4.(a) – 4.(d) and 6, p. 16** in the textbook.

7. Provide other problems as needed for practice.

Workbook Exercise 7, problems 1-2

Activity 2.1d   **Subtract meters and centimeters in compound units**

1. Discuss some subtraction problems where only centimeters are subtracted, and no renaming is necessary.
   - We subtract centimeters from centimeters.

5 m 30 cm – 25 cm = 5 m 5 cm

2. Discuss some problems where centimeters are subtracted and renaming is necessary, such as 5 m 30 cm – 75 cm
   - We can subtract the centimeters from one of the meters, and then add the difference to the remaining centimeters. Subtract 75 cm from one of the meters using mental math techniques for "making 100". 1 m – 75 cm = 25 cm. There is one less meter (4 m). Then add 25 m to the 30 cm already there.

   5 m 30 cm – 75 cm = 4 m 30 cm + 25 cm
   = 4 m 55 cm

   4 m 30 cm   1 m

   - Or, we can rename 1 m 30 cm as 130 cm and subtract 75 cm from 130 cm, using mental techniques or the subtraction algorithm.

   5 m 30 cm – 75 cm
   = 4 m 130 cm – 75 cm
   = 4 m 55 cm

3. Discuss some problems where both centimeters and meters are subtracted, with no renaming.
   - Subtract the meters first, then the centimeters.

   5 m 30 cm – 2 m 25 cm

   $$5\ m\ 30\ cm \xrightarrow{\ -\ 2\ m\ } 3\ m\ 30\ cm \xrightarrow{\ -\ 25\ cm\ } 3\ m\ 5\ cm$$

4. Discuss some problems where both centimeters and meters are subtracted, but renaming is required (not enough centimeters to subtract from).
   - Subtract the meters first.
   - Then subtract the centimeters using the same strategies already learned.
     - Rename 3 m 30 cm to 2 m 130 cm and subtract 75 cm from 130 cm.
     - Or, subtract 75 cm from one of the meters, giving 25 cm, which is added to 30 cm. There is one less meter.

5 m 30 cm – 2 m 75 cm

5 m 30 cm – 2 m 75 cm
= 3 m 30 cm – 75 cm
= 2 m 130 cm – 75 cm
= 2 m 55 cm

or
5 m 30 cm – 2 m 75 cm
= 3 m 30 cm – 75 cm = 2 m 30 cm + 25 cm
                         = 2 m 55 cm
2 m 30 cm   1 m

   - Or, we can write the problem vertically, convert to centimeters, subtract, and then convert back to meters and centimeters. Allow students who are unsure of their mental math abilities to subtract this way. Make sure they include a 0 as a place holder for tens if necessary. For example, 6 m 4 cm needs to be written as 6 m 04 cm or 604 cm.

$$\begin{array}{r} 4\ ^12 \\ \cancel{5}\ \cancel{3}^10\ \text{cm} \\ -\ 2\ 7\ 5\ \text{cm} \\ \hline 2\ 5\ 5\ \text{cm} = 2\ \text{m}\ 55\ \text{cm} \end{array}$$

5. Discuss **task 9.(b), p. 17** in the textbook.

6. Have students do **practice 2A, problems 4.(e) – 4.(h) and 5, p. 16** in the textbook.

7. Provide other problems as needed for practice.

Workbook Exercise 7, problems 3-4

Part 2: Kilometers **3 sessions**

Objectives

- Understand the kilometer as a unit of length.
- Add and subtract kilometers.
- Convert a measurement in kilometers and meters to meters.
- Convert a measurement in meters to kilometers and meters.
- Add and subtract kilometers and meters in compound units.

Materials

- Maps.
- Rulers for each student with centimeter markings.
- String or ribbon.

Homework

- [US]Workbook Exercise 8   [3d]Workbook Exercises 8-10
- [US]Workbook Exercise 9   [3d]Workbook Exercise 11

Notes

The kilometer is the standard unit of measurement in the metric system for longer distances. 1 kilometer = 1000 meters. It is harder for a student to visualize a kilometer than a meter. Find a familiar landmark that is about a kilometer from the school. Find the distances between various cities in kilometers.

U.S. edition: In the U.S. standard system, miles are used to measure longer distances. Your students may be more familiar with miles. A mile is longer than a kilometer. 1 mile equals 1.6093 km, or 1 km equals 0.6214 miles. So a little over half a mile (about six tenths of a mile) is 1 km, 6 miles is about 10 km, and 60 miles is about 100 km. If your students do have some concept of the distance of a mile already, you can use these approximations in order to give your student an idea of what a kilometer is. For example, if the post office is a little over a mile away, you can tell your student it is about 2 km away. A town or landmark about 60 miles (or about an hour's driving time) away is about 100 km away.

Activity 2.2a   **Kilometers**

1. Introduce students to the kilometer as a unit of measurement
   - Refer to **p. 19** in the textbook. Use this page to give students a feeling for the length of a kilometer.
   - Point out that there are 1000 meters in a kilometer. They can imagine 1000 meter sticks lying end-to-end.
   - Use a familiar landmark near the school that is about 1 km away. Draw a roughly scaled map on the board showing the school and the landmark and indicate the distance of 1 km.
   - You can extend this to other distances. Determine the distance to the next city in kilometers.
   - ^{US}Tell your students that a kilometer is a little more than half a mile.

2. Discuss **task 2, p. 20**

3. To help students remember conversion factors for the metric system, you can define the prefixes *centi-, kilo-,*
   - Tell your students that the prefix centi- means a hundred. For example, a *centi*pede has 100 legs. There are 100 *cent*s in a dollar. 100 *centi*meters = 1 meter
   - The prefix kilo- means thousand. 1 *kilo*meter = 1000 meters

4. Discuss converting from kilometers and meters to meters.
   - Remind students that 1 km = 1000 m.
     Write 1 km =1000 m on the board.
   - Ask students for the number of meters in
     - 1 km 500 m
     - 1 km 50 m
     - 1 km 5 m
   - Discuss **task 3, p. 21** in the textbook.
   - Compare this to converting meters and centimeters to centimeters. Students need to remember that 1 kilometer is the same as 1000 meters, but one meter is the same as 100 centimeters.

$$1 \text{ km} = 1000 \text{ m}$$

$$1 \text{ km } 500 \text{ m} = 1500 \text{ m}$$
$$\overset{\diagup \quad \diagdown}{1000 \text{ m} \quad 500 \text{ m}}$$

$$1 \text{ km } 50 \text{ m} = 1050 \text{ m}$$
$$\overset{\diagup \quad \diagdown}{1000 \text{ m} \quad 50 \text{ m}}$$

$$1 \text{ km } 5 \text{ m} = 1005 \text{ m}$$
$$\overset{\diagup \quad \diagdown}{1000 \text{ m} \quad 5 \text{ m}}$$

4. Discuss converting from meters to kilometers and meters.
   - Ask your student for the equivalent number of kilometers for various thousands of meters
   - Discuss **task 1, p. 20** in the textbook.
     - Ask students how they found the answers.
     - You can draw a number-bond diagram for this problem.

$$2000 \text{ m} = \underline{\hspace{1cm}} \text{ km}$$
$$4000 \text{ m} = \underline{\hspace{1cm}} \text{ km}$$
$$10,000 \text{ m} = \underline{\hspace{1cm}} \text{ km}$$

$$1010 \text{ m} = 1 \text{ km } 10 \text{ m}$$
$$\overset{\diagup \quad \diagdown}{1000 \text{ m} \quad 10 \text{ m}}$$

$$1010 \text{ m} + 740 \text{ m} = 1750 \text{ m} = 1 \text{ km } 750 \text{ m}$$
$$\overset{\diagup \quad \diagdown}{1000 \text{ m} \quad 750 \text{ m}}$$

or: 1 km 10 m + 740 m = 2 km 750 m

- Discuss **task 4, p. 21**.

$$400 \text{ m} \times 3 = 1200 \text{ m}$$

$$1200 \text{ m} = 1 \text{ km } 200 \text{ m}$$
$$1000 \text{ m} \quad 200 \text{ m}$$

5. Discuss making 1 km (1000) with meters.
   - Write a problem such as 455 m + ___ m = 1 km.
   - Ask your student how many more meters are needed to make 1 km. They can use mental math strategy of making 1000, since 1 km = 1000 m.
   - Use **Practice 2B, #3, p. 23,** for additional problems to discuss or provide your own.

$$455 \text{ m} + \text{_____} = 1 \text{ km}$$

$$
\begin{aligned}
400 + 500 &= 900 \\
50 + 40 &= 90 \\
5 + 5 &= 10
\end{aligned}
$$

$$455 \text{ m} + 545 \text{ m} = 1 \text{ km}$$

7. Students do **tasks 5-6, p. 21**.

8. For more practice, they can do **Practice 2B, problems 1-3, p. 23.**

Workbook ^{US}Exercise 8 (^{3d}Exercises 8-10)

Activity 2.2b   **Add kilometers and meters in compound units**

1. Discuss some addition problems where only meters are added to kilometers and meters, with the sum of the meters less than 1000.
   - We add the meters together, using mental math strategies or the addition algorithm.

$$2 \text{ km } 650 \text{ m} + 250 \text{ m} = 2 \text{ km } 900 \text{ m}$$

2. Discuss some problems where just meters are added and the sum of the meters is greater than 1000. 1000 m will have to be renamed as 1 km.

   - We can add the meters together, and then convert that sum into kilometers and meters.

$$2 \text{ km } 650 \text{ m} + 750 \text{ m}$$
$$+\, 750 \text{ m}$$
$$2 \text{ m } 650 \text{ cm} \longrightarrow 2 \text{ km } 1400 \text{ m} = 3 \text{ km } 400 \text{ m}$$

   - Or, we can solve this problem by "making 1000" or "making 1 km" with either the 650 m or the 750 m. There will be one more kilometer, and the remainder after making 1000 is the number of meters.

$$2 \text{ km } 650 \text{ m} + 750 \text{ m} = 3 \text{ km } 400 \text{ m}$$
$$350 \text{ cm} \quad 400 \text{ m}$$

   - Or, we can use the addition algorithm. We can convert to meters, add, and then convert back to kilometers and meters.

$$
\begin{array}{r}
{\scriptstyle 1\ 1} \\
2\,6\,5\,0 \ \text{m} \\
+\ \ 7\,5\,0 \ \text{m} \\
\hline
3\,4\,0\,0 \ \text{m} \longrightarrow 3 \text{ km } 400 \text{ m}
\end{array}
$$

3. Discuss some problems where both kilometers and meters are added, and the sum of the meters is less than 1000 (no renaming).
   - Add the kilometers first, then the meters.
   - Meters can be added using mental strategies or the addition algorithm.

$$2 \text{ km } 650 \text{ m} + 3 \text{ km } 75 \text{ m}$$

$$2 \text{ km } 650 \text{ m} \xrightarrow{+3 \text{ km}} 5 \text{ km } 650 \text{ m} \xrightarrow{+75 \text{ m}} 5 \text{ km } 725 \text{ m}$$

4. Discuss some problems where both kilometers and meters are added, and the sum of the meters is more than 1000
   - Add the kilometers first, then the meters.
   - Add the meters using the same strategies already learned.

$$2 \text{ km } 655 \text{ m} + 3 \text{ km } 470 \text{ m}$$

$$2 \text{ km } 655 \text{ m} \xrightarrow{+3 \text{ km}} 5 \text{ km } 655 \text{ m} \xrightarrow{+470 \text{ m}} 6 \text{ km } 125 \text{ m}$$

   - Or, we can convert to meters, add, and convert the sum back to kilometers and meters.

$$8 \text{ km } 789 \text{ m} + 9 \text{ km } 175 \text{ m}$$

```
      1 1
    8 7 8 9  m
 +  9 1 7 5  m
  1 7,9 6 4  m ⟶ 17 km 964 m
```

5. Discuss **p. 22, task 7.(a).**

6. Have students do **practice 2A, problems 4.(a) – 4.(d)** in the textbook.

7. Provide other problems as needed for practice.

Workbook USExercise 9 (3dExercise 11), problems 1-2

Activity 2.2c   **Subtract kilometers and meters in compound units**

1. Discuss some subtraction problems where only meters are subtracted, and no renaming is necessary.
   - We simply subtract meters from meters.

$$5 \text{ km } 130 \text{ m} - 25 \text{ m} = 5 \text{ km } 105 \text{ m}$$

2. Discuss some problems where meters are subtracted and renaming is necessary.

   - We can subtract the meters from one of the kilometers using mental strategies and then add the difference to the remaining meters. Write down one less kilometer, subtract 375 from 1000, and add the difference (625 m) to 130 m.

$$5 \text{ km } 130 \text{ m} - 375 \text{ m} = 4 \text{ km } 130 \text{ m} + 625 \text{ m}$$
$$= 4 \text{ km } 755 \text{ m}$$
$$4 \text{ km } 130 \text{ m } \quad 1 \text{ km}$$

   - Or, we can rename 1 km 130 m as 1130 m and subtract 375 m from 1130 cm, using mental techniques or the subtraction algorithm.

$$5 \text{ km } 130 \text{ m} - 375 \text{ m}$$
$$= 4 \text{ km } 1130 \text{ m} - 375 \text{ m}$$
$$= 4 \text{ km } 755 \text{ m}$$

3. Discuss some problems where both kilometers and meters are subtracted, with no renaming.
   - Subtract the kilometers first, then the meters.

$$5 \text{ km } 500 \text{ m} - 2 \text{ km } 50 \text{ m}$$

$$5 \text{ km } 500 \text{ m} \xrightarrow{-2 \text{ km}} 3 \text{ km } 500 \text{ m} \xrightarrow{-50 \text{ m}} 3 \text{ km } 450 \text{ m}$$

4. Discuss some problems where both kilometers and meters are subtracted, but renaming is required.
   - Subtract the kilometers first, then the meters.
   - Subtract the meters using the same strategies already learned.

$$5 \text{ km } 5 \text{ m} - 2 \text{ km } 450 \text{ m}$$

$$5 \text{ km } 5 \text{ m} \xrightarrow{-2 \text{ km}} 3 \text{ km } 5 \text{ m} \xrightarrow{-450 \text{ m}} 2 \text{ km } 555 \text{ m}$$

   - Students can also use the subtraction algorithm, converting to meters only, and then converting the difference back to kilometers and meters.

$$\begin{array}{r} {\scriptstyle 4 \quad 9} \\ 5\,{}^{1}0\,{}^{1}0\ 5\ \text{m} \\ -\ 2\ 4\ 5\ 0\ \text{m} \\ \hline 2\ 5\ 5\ 5\ \text{m} \longrightarrow 2 \text{ km } 555 \text{ m} \end{array}$$

5. Discuss **task 8, p. 22**.

6. Have students do **practice 2A, problems 4.(e) – 5, p. 23**.

7. Provide other problems as needed for practice.

Workbook ^{US}Exercise 9 (^{3d}Exercise 11), problems 3-4

US**Part 3: Yards, Feet and Inches (pp. 24-26)**	**4 sessions**

Objectives

- Review yards, feet, and inches as units of length.
- Estimate and measure lengths in yards, feet, and inches.
- Convert between yards and feet.
- Convert between feet and inches.
- Add yards, feet, and inches in compound units.
- Subtract yards, feet, and inches in compound units.

Materials

- Meter sticks.
- Yard sticks.
- Rulers for each student with centimeter and inch markings.
- String or ribbon.

Homework

- Workbook Exercise 10
- Workbook Exercise 11, #1-4

Notes

In *Primary Mathematics 2A* students learned about yards, feet, and inches as units of length. Here they will learn to convert between yards, feet, and inches, and to add and subtract in compound units.

Students will not be converting between measurement systems in *Primary Mathematics*, but it is useful for them to have an approximate idea of how they compare. 1 meter is slightly longer than a yard. A centimeter is less than half as long as an inch.

1 inch = 2.54 cm ≈ two and a half centimeters
1 foot = 30.48 cm ≈ 30 cm
1 yard = 0.9144 m ≈ 1 meter
1 meter = 1.0936 yards ≈ 1 yard (≈ 40 in.)

The strategies used here for adding and subtracting in compound units are similar to those used in adding and subtracting metric lengths, except that 1 yard is renamed as 3 feet, and 1 foot is renamed as 12 inches. Renaming in a base other than 10 is good preparation for other instances where the base is not ten; for example, when adding or subtracting hours and minutes or when adding or subtracting whole numbers and fractions. Similar to the strategy of making a 10, we can make a 3 in the case of yards and feet, or make a 12 in the case of feet and inches. Similar to the strategy of subtracting from a ten, which is the next higher place value, we can subtract from a 3 in the case of yards and feet, or subtract from a 12 in the case of feet and inches.

Activity 2.3a **Yards and feet**

1. Refer to the textbook, **p. 24** to review yards, feet, and inches.
   - Have students estimate the lengths of various objects, such as lengths of string or ribbon, to the nearest yard, foot, or inch and then measure.
   - Help your students get an idea of the relationship between the metric measurements and the standard US measurements. Allow your students to use yard sticks, their rulers, or a measuring tape showing both inches and centimeters to answer the following:
     - Which is longer, an inch or a centimeter? (inch)
     - About how much longer? (A little more than twice as long)
     - About how many inches are there in 10 cm? (About 4)
     - In 20 cm? (About 8)
     - In 30 cm? (About 12)
     - About how many centimeters are there in a foot? (About 30)
     - Which is longer, a meter or a yard? (m)
     - How much longer? (About 9 cm or about 3 inches longer)
   - Have your students use yard sticks and rulers and measure something longer than 1 yard to the nearest inch, recording the length in yards, feet, and inches. Students can do this in groups.
   - Lead students to find the relationship (conversion factors) between yards, feet, and inches.
     - Have them use a ruler and a yard stick to determine that 1 foot equals 12 inches and 1 yard equals 36 inches.
     - Ask them how many feet are in 1 yd. There are 3 feet in 1 yard.
     - They need to memorize the number of inches in a foot and feet in a yard.

1 ft = 12 in.
1 yd = 3 ft
1 yd = 36 in.

2. Convert yards to feet.
   - Refer students to the first box in the textbook on **p. 25**.
     - To find the number of feet in a given number of yards, multiply the yards by 3.
     - You can illustrate this with a model showing 3 feet in a yard:

1 yd = 1 x 3 ft = 3 ft
2 yd = 2 x 3 ft = 6 ft
3 yd = 3 x 3 ft = 9 ft
10 yd = 10 x 3 ft = 30 ft
12 yd = 12 x 3 ft = 36 ft
100 yd = 100 x 3 ft = 300 ft

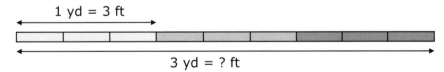

1 yd = 3 ft

3 yd = ? ft

   - Discuss **tasks 1-3, p. 25**.
     - You can illustrate task 3 with number bonds. We multiply the 11 yards by 3 ft to get the number of feet in 11 yards, and then add on the 2 feet.

11 yd 2 ft = 35 ft

11 yd   2 ft

= 11 x 3 ft

= 33 ft

33 ft + 2 ft = 35 ft

- Discuss some other examples, such as:
  - 3 yd 2 ft is _____ ft longer than 3 yards
  - 3 yd 2 ft = _____ ft
  - A rope is 15 yd 2 ft long. What is its length in feet?
- Use **Practice 2C, problem 1, p. 28** for more practice.

3. Convert feet to yards.
   - Refer students to the second box on **p. 25** in the textbook.
   - Discuss **task 4, p. 25**.
   - Ask students to convert a number of feet that is not a multiple of 3 into yards and feet, such as 25 ft.
     - We need to find the number that is closest to 25, but less than 25, that can be divided evenly by 3. We can then separate out the feet into a number that can be divided by 3, and the rest. We divide 24 by 3 to get the number of yards.

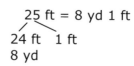

     - You can illustrate this with a scale drawing, showing the feet, and marking yards one by one. 24 feet are used up to make 8 yards, and there is one foot left over.

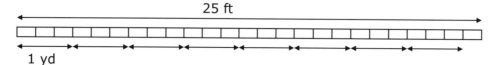

     - Point out that this process is similar to dividing with remainders. We can divide 25 by 3. The quotient is the number of yards, and the remainder is the number of feet.

$$\begin{array}{r} 8 \\ 3\overline{)25} \\ 24 \\ \hline 1 \end{array}$$

25 ft = 8 yd 1 ft

   - Provide some other examples, such as:
     - 95 ft = _____ yd _____ ft.
     - A couch is 10 ft long. How long is it in yards and feet?

   - Use **Practice 2C, problem 3, p. 28** for more practice.

4. Subtracting feet from one yard.
   - Tell your students you have a yard of rope and need to cut off 1 foot of rope. Ask how many feet are left. There are 2 feet left, since there are 3 feet in a yard. Write the problem as a subtraction equation.

1 yd – 1 ft = 2 ft

   - Now tell them you have 2 yards and need to cut off 1 yard and 2 feet of rope. Ask how many more feet are left. We just need to go up to the next yard from 1 yd 1 ft to get to 2 yd. So we can just count up from the number of feet to 3. There are 2 ft left.

2 yd – 1 yd 1 ft = 2 ft

   - Use **Practice 2C, problems 5(a) – 5.(c), p. 28** for more practice.

Workbook ᵁˢExercise 10, problems 1-2

Activity 2.3b   **Feet and inches**

1. Convert feet to inches.
   - Refer students to the third box on **p. 25** in the textbook.
     - o   To convert feet into inches we multiply the given number of feet by 12.
     - o   You can lay 12 inch (foot) rulers side by side to illustrate.
   - Expand the table to 10 ft.   Use it to work on memorizing the facts for multiplication by 12.
     - o   Have students practice counting by 12's.   They can count up one ten, and then up 2 ones.
     - o   Say the number of feet and call on students to give the number of inches.
     - o   Students may also use mental math strategies for multiplying 12 by a single digit:
       $$12 \times 8 = 80 + 16 = 96$$
   - Discuss **tasks 5-7, p. 25**.   You can have several students measure the door for task 7 and have the rest find the width in inches.

1 ft = 1 x 12 in. = 12 in.
2 ft = 2 x 12 in. = 24 in.
3 ft = 3 x 12 in. = 36 in.
4 ft = 4 x 12 in. = 48 in.
5 ft = 5 x 12 in. = 60 in.
6 ft = 6 x 12 in. = 72 in.
7 ft = 7 x 12 in. = 84 in.
8 ft = 8 x 12 in. = 96 in.
9 ft = 9 x 12 in. = 108 in.
10 ft = 10 x 12 in. = 120 in.

   - Provide a few other problems for practice, such as:
     - o   How many inches are in a yard?
     - o   I am 5 ft 4 in. tall. How tall am I in inches?
   - Use **Practice 2C, problem 2, p. 28** for more practice.

3. Convert from inches to feet and inches.
   (Note: students have not yet learned to divide by a 2-digit number. All problems at this level involving the conversion of inches to feet will use small multiples of 12 such as 24 or 36, plus a few inches. Students should be able to determine the number of feet and inches by the multiplication facts for 12 x 2 = 24 and 12 x 3 = 36. They can count up by 12s).
   - Ask student to convert 15 inches to feet and inches.
     - o   12 inches = 1 foot; 15 – 12 = 3 inches are left over.

       15 in. = 1 ft 3 in.
       12 in.   3 in.
   - Provide a few more problems using a few inches more than 24 or 36 only.
     - o   Find the number of feet and inches in 40 inches.
     - o   A ribbon is 30 in. long. What is its length in feet?
   - Use **Practice 2C, problem 4, p. 28** for more practice.

4. Subtract inches from feet.
   - Give your student a number of inches less than 12 and ask them to tell you the number of inches needed to make a foot. Repeat with all the numbers 1-11 randomly. They need to "make a 12" or "make a foot."
   - Write some subtraction equations involving subtracting inches from 1 foot.

     1 ft – 8 in. = 4 in.
   - Have students solve some subtraction equations involving finding the number of inches to get to the next foot, such as 3 ft – 2 ft 10 inches = 2 inches.

     3 ft – 2 ft 10 in. = 2 in.
   - Use **Practice 2C, problems 5.(d)-5.(e), 28** for more practice.

Workbook ᵁˢExercise 10, problems 3-5

Activity 2.3c   **Add or subtract yards and feet in compound units**

1. Discuss strategies for adding feet.
   - Have your student add 1 foot + 1 foot, 1 foot + 2 feet, and 2 feet + 2 feet, and convert the answer into yards and feet where appropriate.
   - Point out that with 2 ft + 2 ft, we can mentally make a 3 with 2 ft by taking 1 ft from the 2 ft we are adding, which gives us 1 yd and 1 ft.

   1 ft + 1 ft = 2 ft
   1 ft + 2 ft = 3 ft = 1 yd
   2 ft + 2 ft = 4 ft = 1 yd 1 ft
   2 ft + 2 ft = 1 yd 1 ft
       1 ft   1 ft

2. Discuss strategies for adding yards and feet in compound units.
   - Add yards first. Then add the feet. If there are 3 ft or more, rename each 3 feet as 1 yard and write the new answer.

     3 yd 1 ft + 2 yd 1 ft = 5 yd 2 ft

   - As students become familiar with adding yards and feet, they can omit the intermediate step by looking ahead to see if adding the feet will result in a sum larger than 3, and therefore another yard. If it does not, write the sum for the yards. If it does, increase the sum for the yards by 1.

     3 yd 2 ft + 2 yd 1 ft = 5 yd 3 ft = 6 yd

     3 yd 2 ft + 2 yd 2 ft = 5 yd 4 ft = 6 yd 1 ft

   - Since we are working with fairly small numbers of feet, we could add the feet first and remember the result.
     - If the sum of the feet is 1 or 2, then we just add the yards, write that down, and write the number of feet.
     - If the sum of the feet is 3, we add the yards and increase the sum by 1.
     - If the sum of the feet is 4, we add the yards, increase it by 1, and write 1 for the feet.
   - We can also write the problem vertically and add feet first, renaming 3 feet as 1 yard. (This is similar to the addition algorithm, except that in the addition algorithm ten ones are renamed as a ten.)

3. Discuss strategies for subtracting just feet from yards and feet.
   - Have students subtract 2 ft from 3 yd 1 ft.
     - We can rename 1 yd 1 ft as 4 ft, and then subtract 2 ft to get 2 ft.
     - Or, we can subtract 2 ft from 1 of the yards, giving 1 ft, and add that to the remaining yards and feet.

     3 yd 1 ft – 2 ft = 2 yd 4 ft – 2 ft
                      = 2 yd 2 ft

     3 yd 1 ft – 2 ft = 2 yd 1 ft + 1 ft
                      = 2 yd 2 ft
     2 yd 1 ft   1 yd

4. Discuss strategies for subtracting both yards and feet in compound units.
   - Subtract yards first, then feet
     - Write an intermediate step or look ahead to see whether subtracting the feet results in 1 less yard.
     - Subtract the feet using strategies already learned.
   - We can also write the problem vertically, and subtract feet first, renaming if necessary.

     5 yd 2 ft – 2 yd 1 ft = 3 yd 1 ft

     5 yd 2 ft – 2 yd 2 ft = 3 yd 2 ft – 2 ft
                      = 3 yd

     5 yd 1 ft – 2 yd 2 ft = 3 yd 1 ft – 2 ft
                      = 2 yd 2 ft

        19   3
        2̶0̶ yd
     –   7 yd   2 ft
        12 yd   1 ft

5. Use **Practice 2C, problem 6, p. 28** for more practice.

6. Give students a word problem to solve, such as the following. They can draw a diagram.

   Brett had two sticks. The first one was 4 yd 1 ft long and the second one was 2 yd 2 ft long. How much longer is the first one than the second one?

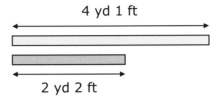

4 yd 1 ft

2 yd 2 ft

4 yd 1 ft – 2 yd 2 ft = 1 yd 2 ft
It is 1 yd 2 ft longer.

Activity 2.3d　　　　　　**Add or subtract feet and inches in compound units**

1. Discuss strategies for adding inches.
   - We can add the inches and then convert to feet and inches.
   - We can make a 12 (1 foot), taking inches from one of the numbers of inches to make 12 with the other. The remainder is the number of inches.

   11 in. + 8 in. = 19 in. = 1 ft 7 in.
   　　　　　　　12 in. 　7 in.

   11 in. + 8 in. = 1 ft 7 in.
   　　1 in. 　7 in.

2. Discuss strategies for adding feet and inches.
   - You can use **task 8.(a), p. 26**
   - We can add the feet first, and then add the inches using strategies already learned.

   - Or, we can rewrite the problem vertically, add inches, rename 12 inches as 1 foot, and add feet.

   4 ft 7 in. + 1 ft 10 in.
   = 5 ft 7 in. + 10 in. = 6 ft 5 in.
   　　　　5 in. 　5 in.

   $$\begin{array}{r} \overset{1}{}\\ 4 \text{ ft} \quad 7 \text{ in.}\\ +\ \underline{1 \text{ ft} \quad 10 \text{ in.}}\\ 6 \text{ ft.} \quad 5 \text{ in.} \end{array}$$ (7 in.+10 in. = 1 ft 5 in.)

3. Discuss strategies for subtracting inches from feet and inches.
   - Have students subtract 9 in. from 3 ft 5 in. There are not enough inches to subtract from.
     - We can convert 1 foot to 12 inches, so we now have 17 in., and can subtract 9 in.
     - Or, can subtract 9 in. from one of the feet. We now have one less foot and 3 more inches. We add the 3 inches to the 5 inches we already have.

   3 ft 5 in. – 9 in. = 2 ft 17 in. – 9 in.
   　　　　　　　　　= 2 ft. 8 in.

   3 ft 5 in. – 9 in. = 2 ft 5 in. + 3 in.
   　　　　　　　　　　= 2 ft. 8 in.
   2 ft 5 in. 　1 ft.

4. Discuss strategies for subtracting feet and inches.
   - You can use **p. 26, task 8.(b)**.
   - We can subtract the feet first, and then subtract the inches using strategies we have already learned.
   - We can rewrite the problem vertically, rename 1 ft as 12 in if necessary, subtract the inches, and then subtract the feet.

4 ft 7 in. – 1 ft 10 in. = 3 ft 7 in. – 10 in.
= 2 ft 9 in.

$$\begin{array}{r} \overset{3}{\cancel{4}}\text{ ft } \overset{19}{\cancel{7}}\text{ in.} \\ -\quad 1\text{ ft } 10\text{ in.} \\ \hline 2\text{ ft } \;\,9\text{ in.} \end{array}$$

5. Have students do **Practice 2C, problem 7, p. 28**.

6. Discuss some additional word problems, such as the following:

   - Amy has two pieces of yarn. The green yarn is 5 ft 8 in. long and the red yarn is 2 ft 10 in. long. Find the total length of the two pieces of yarn.

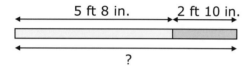

5 ft 8 in. + 2 ft 10 in. = 8 ft 6 in.
The total length is 8 ft 6 in.

   - John has a board that is 6 ft 3 in. long. How long is the board after he saws off 30 inches? Give your answer in feet and inches.

30 inches = 2 ft 6 in
6 ft 3 in. – 2 ft 6 in. = 3 ft 9 in
He needs to saw off 3 ft 9 in.

or

6 ft 3 in. – 30 in. = 3 ft 39 in. – 30 in.
= 3 ft 9 in.

3 ft 36 in.

   - It is 12 ft 4 inches from the back door of a kitchen to an arch between the kitchen and the living room. It is 24 ft 8 inches from this arch to a window in the living room. How far is it from the back door to the window in the living room? Give your answer in feet and inches.

12 ft 4 in. + 24 ft 8 in. = 36 ft 12 in. = 12 yd 1 ft
It is 12 yd 1 ft from the back door to the window.

Workbook ᵘˢExercise 11, problems 1-4

US Part 4: Miles	1 session

Objectives

- Understand the mile as a unit of length.
- Add and subtract miles.

Materials

- Maps with distances marked in miles.

Homework

- Workbook Exercise 11, #5-6

Notes

In the U.S., distances are measured in miles rather than in kilometers.

A mile is longer than a kilometer; 1 mile equals 1.6093 km.

This session is short; you can use the opportunity to do some review of previous lessons or to catch up, or you can combine this session with the next review session.

Activity 2.4a   **Miles**

1. Familiarize your students with miles.
   - Tell your students that in the US we use miles rather than kilometers to measure distances. Your students are probably familiar with miles.
   - Discuss some distances in miles to known landmarks or between known landmarks. You can draw a roughly scaled map and mark the distances in miles.
   - You may wish to relate miles to kilometers. A mile is a little longer than one and a half miles. So a distance of 100 kilometers, for example, is about 60 miles.
   - Discuss **p. 27** in the textbook.
     - Students should try to memorize 1 mile = 5280 feet.
   - This is a good place to introduce a few important facts.
     - The distance around the earth at the equator is about 25,000 miles
     - The highest mountain is about 5 miles high.
     - The deepest trench is about 10 miles deep.
     - The distance from the North Pole to the South Pole through the center of the earth is about 8,000 miles.

2. Add or subtract miles.

   - Have students do **tasks 1-2** on **p. 27**.
   - You can discuss a few additional problems, such as:

     - By air, the distance between Atlanta and Dallas is 800 miles. The distance between Atlanta and El Paso is 1450 miles. What is the distance between Dallas and El Paso?

       You can have your students diagram the information:

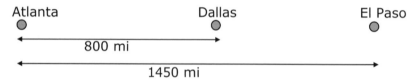

       Distance between Dallas and El Paso = 1450 mi – 800 mi = 650 mi.

       How many miles would you fly if you took a round trip from El Paso to Atlanta?

       Total distance = 1450 mi + 1450 mi = 2900 mi

     - It is 1390 miles when you fly from Boston to Minneapolis and 1650 miles when you fly from Minneapolis to Seattle. How far is it from Boston to Seattle if the flight stops over in Minneapolis?

       1390 mi + 1650 mi = 3040 mi
       It is 3040 miles from Boston to Seattle

     - How much further is it from Minneapolis to Seattle than from Minneapolis to Boston?

       1650 mi – 1390 mi = 260 mi
       It is 260 miles further to Seattle than to Boston.

Workbook ᵁˢExercise 11, problems 5-6

^{US}**Practice**	**1 session**

Objectives

- Practice calculations and word problems involving U.S. standard measurements.
- Solve word problems.

Materials

- Practice sets (in this guide).

Activity 2.5a   **Review**

- Use any **Practice 2C** problems not already done.

- You can use the worksheets on the next few pages for additional review. Answers are given here.

Answers for Practice Set 1

1. (a) 32 ft   (b) 19 ft   (c) 36 ft   (d) 452 ft
2. (a) 47 in.   (b) 116 in.   (c) 125 in.   (d) 94 in.
3. (a) 1 ft 5 in. (b) 4 ft 0 in. (c) 2 ft 2 in.
4. (a) 6 yd 2 ft   (c) 14 yd 0 ft (c) 68 yd 2 ft (d) 133 yd 1 ft
5. (a) 2 ft   (b) 1 ft   (c) 7 in.   (d) 9 in.   (e) 3 in.
6. (a) 2 ft 5 in., 39 in., 4 ft, 1 yd 2 ft
   (b) 1500 yd, 5000 ft, 1 mi

Answers for Practice Set 2

1. (a) 3 ft 4 in.   (b) 4 ft 8 in.   (c) 5 ft 3 in.   (d) 6 yd 1 ft
   (e) 11 yd 1 ft   (f) 20 yd 2 ft   (g) 31 yd 1 ft   (h) 10 ft 6 in.
   (i) 12 ft 0 in. (j) 20 ft 5 in.

2. (a) 3 ft 2 in.   (b) 5 ft 9 in.   (c) 9 ft 11 in.   (d) 6 yd 0 ft
   (e) 7 yd 2 ft   (f) 2 yd 1 ft   (g) 11 yd 2 ft   (h) 11 yd 2 ft
   (i) 4 ft 4 in.   (j) 7 ft 1 in.

Answers for Practice Set 3

1. (a) 18 ft   (b) 84 in.   (c) 34 in.
   (d) 79 in.   (e) 325 ft   (f) 131 ft

2. (a) 8 yd 1 ft   (b) 68 yd 0 ft   (c) 104 yd 2 ft
   (d) 33 yd 1 ft   (e) 1 ft 4 in.   (f) 2 ft 2 in.

3. (a) 1 ft   (b) 4 in.   (c) 7 in.   (d) 6 in.
4. (a) 1 ft 10 in. (b) 16 yd 0 ft   (c) 10 yd 2 ft
   (d) 7 yd 2 ft   (e) 8 ft 11 in.   (f) 159 yd 1 ft 5 in.

5. (a) <   (b) >   (c) <   (d) =

Practice Set 1

1. (a)   10 yd 2 ft = _____ ft

    (b)   6 yd 1 ft = _____ ft

    (c)   12 yd = _____ ft

    (d)   150 yd 2 ft = _____ ft

2. (a) 3 ft 11 in. = _____ in.

    (b) 9 ft 8 in. = _____ in.

    (c) 10 ft 5 in. = _____ in.

    (d) 7 ft 10 in. = _____ in.

3. (a) 17 in. = _____ ft _____ in.

    (b) 48 in. = _____ ft _____ in.

    (c) 26 in. = _____ ft _____ in.

4. (a) 20 ft = _____ yd _____ ft

    (b) 42 ft = _____ yd _____ ft

    (c) 206 ft = _____ yd _____ ft

    (d) 400 ft = _____ yd _____ ft

5. (a) 4 yd – 3 yd 1 ft = _____ ft

    (b) 12 yd – 11 yd 2 ft = _____ ft

    (c) 1 ft – 5 in. = _____ in.

    (d) 2 ft – 1 ft 3 in. = _____ in.

    (e) 10 ft – 9 ft 9 in. = _____ in.

6. Put in order from shortest to longest.

    (a) 1 yd 2 ft   4 ft   39 in.   2 ft 5 in.

    (b) 1500 yd   1 mi   5000 ft

Practice Set 2

1. Add in compound units

   (a) 2 ft 11 in. + 5 in. = _____ ft _____ in.

   (b) 3 ft 9 in. + 11 in. = _____ ft _____ in.

   (c) 4 ft 7 in. + 8 in. = _____ ft _____ in.

   (d) 5 yd 2 ft + 2 ft = _____ yd _____ ft

   (e) 6 yd 2 ft + 4 yd 2 ft = _____ yd _____ ft

   (f) 8 yd 1 ft + 12 yd 1 ft = _____ yd _____ ft

   (g) 12 yd 2 ft + 18 yd 2 ft = _____ yd _____ ft

   (h) 6 ft 9 in. + 3 ft 9 in. = _____ ft _____ in.

   (i) 3 ft 8 in. + 8 ft 4 in. = _____ ft _____ in.

   (j) 13 ft 11 in. + 6 ft 6 in. = _____ ft _____ in.

2. Subtract in compound units

   (a) 3 ft 8 in. – 6 in. = _____ ft _____ in.

   (b) 6 ft 4 in. – 7 in. = _____ ft _____ in.

   (c) 10 ft 5 in. – 6 in. = _____ ft _____ in.

   (d) 6 yd 1 ft – 1 ft = _____ yd _____ ft

   (e) 8 yd 1 ft – 2 ft = _____ yd _____ ft

   (f) 7 yd 2 ft – 5 yd 1 ft = _____ yd _____ ft

   (g) 13 yd 1 ft – 1 yd 2 ft = _____ yd _____ ft

   (h) 18 yd 1 ft – 6 yd 2 ft = _____ yd _____ ft

   (i) 7 ft 3 in. – 2 ft 11 in. = _____ ft _____ in.

   (j) 12 ft 10 in. – 5 ft 9 in. = _____ ft _____ in.

Practice Set 3

1. Write in feet or inches.

   (a) 6 yd = _____ ft   (b) 7 ft = _____ in.

   (c) 2 ft 10 in. = _____ in.   (d) 6 ft 7 in. = _____ in.

   (e) 108 yd 1 ft = _____ ft   (f) 43 yd 2 ft = _____ ft

2. Write in compound units.

   (a) 25 ft = _____ yd _____ ft   (b) 204 ft = _____ yd _____ ft

   (c) 314 ft = _____ yd _____ ft   (d) 100 ft = _____ yd _____ ft

   (e) 16 in. = _____ ft _____ in.   (f) 26 in. = _____ ft _____ in.

3. Subtract.

   (a) 1 yd – 2 ft = _____ ft   (b) 1 ft – 8 in. = _____ in.

   (c) 42 ft – 41 ft 5 in. = _____ in.   (d) 1 yd – 2 ft 6 in. = _____ in.

4. Add or subtract.

   (a) 12 ft 9 in. – 10 ft 11 in. = _____ ft _____ in.

   (b) 15 yd 1 ft + 2 ft = _____ yd _____ ft

   (c) 14 yd 1 ft – 3 yd 2 ft = _____ yd _____ ft

   (d) 12 yd 2 ft – 5 yd = _____ yd _____ ft

   (e) 15 ft 1 in. – 6 ft 2 in. = _____ ft _____ in.

   (f) 344 ft 11 in. + 133 ft 6 in. = _____ yd _____ ft _____ in.

5. Put >, <, or = in the circles.

   (a) 1 mile $\bigcirc$ 5820 feet   (b) 1 inch $\bigcirc$ 1 centimeter

   (c) 1 yard $\bigcirc$ 1 meter   (d) 1 yard $\bigcirc$ 36 inches

Unit 3 – Weight

Objectives
- Review kilograms and grams.
- Convert between kilograms and grams.
- Add or subtract kilograms and grams in compound units.
- Solve word problems involving weight in kilograms and grams using part-whole and comparison models.
- [US]Review pounds and ounces.
- [US]Convert between pounds and ounces.
- [US]Add or subtract pounds and ounces in compound units.

Suggested number of sessions: 9

	Objectives	Textbook	Workbook	Activities
Part 1 : Kilograms and Grams				**3 sessions**
22	• Review kilograms and grams. • Read scales. • Estimate and weigh objects.	[US]pp. 29-30 [3d]pp. 24-25	Ex. 12	3.1a
23	• Convert between kilograms and grams. • Subtract grams from 1 kilogram.	[US]pp. 30-31, 33 [3d]pp. 25-26, 28 Practice 3A, #1-3	[US]Ex. 13 [3d]Ex. 13-14	3.1b
24	• Add or subtract kilograms and grams in compound units.	[US]pp. 32-33 [3d]pp. 27-28 Practice 3A, #4-5	[US]Ex. 14 [3d]Ex. 15	3.1c
Part 2 : More Word Problems				**2 sessions**
25	• Solve word problems involving weight using part-whole or comparison models.	[US]pp. 34-37 [3d]pp. 29-32	[US]Ex. 15 [3d]Ex. 16	3.2a
26	• Practice.	[US]p. 38 [3d]p. 33		3.2b
[US]**Part 3 : Pounds and Ounces**				**4 sessions**
27	• Review pounds and ounces. • Read scales in pounds and ounces. • Estimate and weigh objects.	[US]pp. 39-40		3.3a
28	• Convert between pounds and grams. • Subtract ounces from 1 pound.	[US]p. 40, 42 [US]Practice 3C, #1-2		3.1b
29	• Add or subtract pounds and ounces in compound units.	[US]pp. 41-42 [US]Practice 3C, #3-7	[US]Ex. 16	3.1c
30	• Practice.			3.1d

Part 1: Kilograms and Grams | **3 sessions**

Objectives

- Review kilograms and grams.
- Estimate and weigh in kilograms and grams.
- Read scales.
- Convert between kilograms and grams.
- Add and subtract kilograms and grams in compound units

Materials

- Kilogram weights.
- Various gram weights.
- Various canned foods or other items that have the weight marked in grams.
- Various types of weighing scales.
- A balance.
- Objects that can be weighed.
- Pennies, paper clips.

Homework

- [US]Workbook Exercise 12
- [US]Workbook Exercise 13   [3d]Workbook Exercises 13-14
- [US]Workbook Exercise 14   [3d]Workbook Exercise 15

Notes

The standard units, kilograms and grams, were introduced in *Primary Mathematics 2A*. Students weighed objects and read scales in either kilograms or grams. Here they will weigh objects in compound units, kilograms and grams. Students will also learn to add and subtract in compound units. The process is the similar to adding and subtracting kilometers and meters.

Give students practical work in measuring weight, and in using different weighing scales. Encourage them to estimate a weight before measuring it. Estimation will give the students a better understanding of the units.

Remark, for teachers only: Strictly speaking, the kilogram is a unit of mass (a measure of the amount of matter in the object), not of weight (a measure of the force of gravity on an object). However, since we use the term weight in daily speech when weighing things, it will be used here.

A quart (or liter) of water weighs about 1 kg. Four hundred pennies weigh about 1 kg.

Two regular paper clips weigh about 1 gram. The unit cube in some base-10 sets weighs 1 gram. A teaspoon of water weighs 5 grams. Many food products have weight marked both in kilograms and grams and in the U.S. in pounds and ounces as well.

[US]On earth, a kilogram weighs 2.2 pounds, that is, a bit over two pounds. A good estimate when given the weight of a person in kilograms, for someone used to pounds, is to double that weight. So when the textbook says a person weighs 30 kilograms, then that person weighs about 60 pounds (and is likely a child).

Activity 3.1a   **Weigh in kilograms and grams**

1. Review kilograms.
   - Show your students a 1-kilogram weight. Remind them that the kilogram is a standard unit of weight.
   - Have them take turns handling the weight and feeling how heavy it is.
   - Have students estimate the weight of various objects by feel as being about 1 kg, less than 1 kg, or more than 1 kg, and then verify with a balance.

2. Review grams.
   - Show your student various gram weights. Remind them that the gram is also a unit of weight. It is quite light. About 2 paper clips weigh a gram.
   - Have students take turns handling some gram weights. You can also have them feel the weight of some objects marked in grams, such as canned food.
   - If you discussed prefixes, ask students if they remember what *kilo-* means. It means a thousand. Ask them if they can figure out how many grams are in a kilogram from the prefix. There are 1000 grams in 1 kilogram.

   $$1 \text{ kg} = 1000 \text{ g}$$

3. Read scales.
   - Put an object on a scale and have the students observe the pointer going around.
   - Discuss the divisions on the weighing scales shown in the textbook, ^{US}**p. 29 (^{3d}p. 24)**.
     - Lead students to see that if 1 kg is divided into 10 equal parts, each part stands for 100 g and if is divided into 20 equal parts, each part stands for 50 g.
     - Ask students questions about the scale, such as
       - What is the largest division marked off? (1 kg).
       - What is the next largest division? (500 g)
       - There are 5 markings between every 500 g. What does each such mark stand for? (100 g)
       - What are the next larger divisions? (50 g)
       - What are the smallest divisions? (10 g)
       - We can determine that the package weighs 650 gram by first looking for the closest written weight (500 g) to the pointer, and counting up first by 100s, and then by 50s, until we get to the mark the pointer is pointing to.
       - What if the pointer pointed to 1 kg? How many grams is that? (1000 g). 2kg? (2000 g)

         1 kg 300 g = 1300 g

       - Have students supply the answers for the two other scales on ^{US}**p. 30 (^{3d}p. 25)**.

         1000 g   300 g

       - Have students give the weight of the papaya in grams.
   - Have students supply the answers for **task 1, ^{US}p. 30 (^{3d}p. 25)**.

4. Students estimate and weigh objects.
   - Divide students in groups.
   - Give each group some objects that weigh over 1 kg and have them estimate and then weigh them. Be sure that the scale or weighing machine the group is using can weigh the objects. If the scale only goes up to 4 g, give them objects that weigh between 1 and 4 g.

Object	Weight	
	kg	g
	kg	g
	kg	g

   - Students should record their measurements in a table.

- Groups can exchange objects and measure the weight of each object.
- You may want to combine this with problem #1 in exercise 12, since students may not be able to do this problem as homework if they do not have scales which measure in kilograms and grams at home.

Workbook Exercise 12

Activity 3.1b   **Kilograms and grams**

1. Discuss converting between kilograms and grams.
   - Remind students that 1 kg = 1000 g. Write 1 kg = 1000 g on the board.
   - Discuss textbook, **task 2-3, ^{US}p. 30 (^{3d}p. 25)**.
   - Have students find the answers for **Practice 3A, problem 1, ^{US}p. 33 (^{3d}p. 28)**.

   - Discuss textbook, **task 3, ^{US}p. 30 (^{3d}p. 25)**.
   - Have students find the answers for **Practice 3A, problem 2, ^{US}p. 33 (^{3d}p. 28)**.

$$1 \text{ kg} = 1000 \text{ g}$$

$$2 \text{ kg } 200 \text{ g} = 2200 \text{ g}$$
$$2000 \text{ g} \qquad 200 \text{ g}$$

$$350 \text{ g} \times 4 = 1400 \text{ g}$$
$$1400 \text{ g} = 1 \text{ kg } 400 \text{ g}$$
$$1000 \text{ g} \qquad 400 \text{ g}$$

2. Discuss making 1 kg with grams.
   - Write a problem such as 455 g + _____ g = 1 kg.
   - Ask your student how many more grams are needed to make 1 kg. They can use mental math strategies for making 1000.
   - Rewrite the problem as a subtraction problem.
   - Rewrite the problem by adding 2 kg to both values. Students should see that they are still "making 1000" or finding the difference between the grams and the next kilogram.
   - Discuss textbook, **tasks 4-6, ^{US}p. 31 (^{3d}p. 26)**.
   - Use **Practice 3A, #3, ^{US}p. 33 (^{3d}p. 28)**, for additional problems to discuss or have the students solve them independently.

$$455 \text{ g} + \underline{\hspace{2cm}} = 1 \text{ kg}$$

$$1 \text{ kg} - 455 \text{ g} = \underline{\hspace{2cm}}$$

$$3 \text{ kg} - 2 \text{ kg } 455 \text{ g} = \underline{\hspace{2cm}}$$

Workbook ^{US}Exercise 13 (^{3d}Exercises 13-14)

Activity 3.1c   **Add and subtract kilograms and grams in compound units**

1. Discuss addition of kilograms and grams in compound units.
   - The same strategies that were learned for adding kilometers and meters in compound units can be used here. If your students are still weak with this, start with some problems where they are just adding grams to kilograms and grams where the sum of the grams is less than 1000, then do some problems where the sum of the grams is greater than 1000, and then some where they are adding both kilograms and grams.

- Discuss **task 7(a), ^{US}p. 32 (^{3d}p. 27).**
  - o Add the kilograms first.

  - o Add the grams.

    - We can make 1 kg (1000 g) with the 960 g using 40 g.

    - Or, we can add the grams to get 1040 g and then rename as 1 kg 40 g.

3 kg 80 g + 1 kg 960 g

$$3 \text{ kg } 80 \text{ g} \xrightarrow{\;+ 1 \text{ kg}\;} 4 \text{ kg } 80 \text{ g}$$

$$4 \text{ kg } 80 \text{ g} \xrightarrow{\;+ 960 \text{ kg}\;} 5 \text{ kg } 40 \text{ g}$$

4 kg 80 g + 960 g = 5 kg 40 g
40 g   40 g

4 kg 80 g + 960 g
= 4 kg + 1040 g
= 5 kg 40 g

2. Discuss subtraction of kilograms and grams in compound units.
   - The same strategies that were learned for subtracting kilometers and meters in compound units can be used here.
   - Show a problem such as 2 kg 300 g – 750 g. Discuss strategies for subtraction.
     - o We can split 2 kg 300 g into 1 kg 300 g and 1 kg, then subtract 750 g from 1 kg (100 g) and then add the difference (250 g) to 1 kg 300 g.

     - o Or, we can rename 1 kg 300 g as 1300 g and subtract 750 g.

2 kg 300 g – 750 g = 1 kg 300 g + 250 g
1 kg 300 g   1 kg   = 1 kg 550 g

2 kg 300 g – 750 g
= 1 kg 1300 g – 750 g
= 1 kg 550 g

- Discuss **task 7(b), ^{US}p. 32 (^{3d}p. 27).**
  - o Subtract the kilograms, then the grams.

- Use **Practice 3A, #4-6, ^{US}p. 33 (^{3d}p. 28),** for additional problems. They can be discussed as a class, or students can solve them individually and then explain their method.

3 kg 80 g – 1 kg 960 g

$$3 \text{ kg } 80 \text{ g} \xrightarrow{\;- 1 \text{ kg}\;} 2 \text{ kg } 80 \text{ g}$$

$$2 \text{ kg } 80 \text{ g} \xrightarrow{\;- 960 \text{ g}\;} 1 \text{ kg } 120 \text{ g}$$

Workbook ^{US}Exercise 14 (^{3d}Exercise 15)

Part 2: More Word Problems   **2 sessions**

Objectives

- Solve word problems involving weight using the part-whole and comparison models.

Homework

- ^{US}Workbook Exercise 15 ^{3d}Workbook Exercise 16

Notes

Pictorial models as a tool for solving word problems were introduced in *Primary Mathematics 3A*. Two basic types of models used are a part-whole model using one bar to represent the total, and a comparison model using two or more bars to represent the quantities being compared. See the examples below.

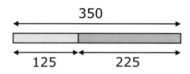

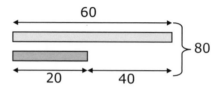

- Given two parts, 125 and 225, we can find the whole by addition. 125 + 225 = 350
- Given a whole (350) and a part (125), we can find the other part by subtraction. 350 – 125 = 225

- Given the two quantities being compared (60 and 20), we can find the difference by subtraction. 60 – 20 = 40.
- Given the smaller quantity (20) and the difference (40), we can find the larger quantity by addition. 20 + 40 = 60.
- Given the larger quantity (60) and the difference (40), we can find the smaller quantity by subtraction. 60 – 40 = 20
- Once both quantities have been found, we can find the total by addition. 60 + 20 = 80
- Given the total (80) and the larger quantity (60), we can find the smaller quantity by subtraction. 80 – 60 = 20. Once we find the smaller quantity, we can find the difference by subtraction. 60 – 20 = 40

The part-whole and comparison models are also used with multiplication and division. Each part of equal value is called a **unit**. The comparison model is used for problems involving how many times as many or how many times more one quantity is than another.

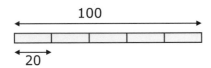

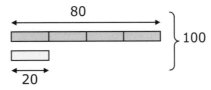

- Given the total (100) and the number of units (5), we can find the value of a unit by division. $100 \div 5 = 20$
- Given the value of a unit (20) and the number of units (5), we can find the total by multiplication. $20 \times 5 = 100$

- Given the value of the smaller quantity (20) and how many times as much the larger quantity is compared to the smaller quantity 4 times larger), we can find the larger quantity by multiplication. $20 \times 4 = 80$
- Given the larger quantity (80) and how many times as much it is compared to the smaller quantity (4 times), we can find smaller quantity by division. $80 \div 4 = 20$
- Once we know the value of one unit, we can find each quantity.

These models can be combined to illustrate more complicated problems.

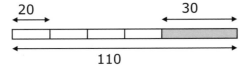

- Given the value of a unit (20), the number of units (4), and another part (30), we can find the total by multiplication and then addition. $20 \times 4 = 80$, $90 + 30 = 110$
- Given the value of a unit (20), the number of units (4), and the total (80), we can find the part by multiplication and then subtraction. $20 \times 4 = 80$, $110 - 80 = 30$
- Given the total (110), the part (30), and the number of units (4) in the other part, we can find the value of the unit by subtraction, and then division. $110 - 30 = 80$, $80 \div 4 = 20$

Students should become proficient at drawing models when needed, but are not required to draw a model for every exercise problem if they can solve the problem without a drawing. However, you may have to continue requiring model drawing for all problems until students are no longer making mistakes in their equations.

Activity 3.2a   **Solve word problems using models**

1. Discuss using part-whole models to solve word problems.
   - Refer to [US]p. 34 ([3d]p. 29) in the textbook.
   - Draw the model one step at a time on the board and relate each part to a specific part of the problem.
   - Ask students questions as you model the problem. For example:
     - What do we need to find? The weight of the marbles.
     - What do we know? The weight of the empty jar.
     - What else do we know? The weight of the jar and the marbles. Draw a bar to show the total weight.
     - How many parts do we have? Two, the weight of the empty jar and the weight of the marbles.
     - Which is likely to be smaller? The weight of the jar. Divide the bar into two parts, a shorter part and a longer part and label the shorter part with the weight of the jar.
     - Do we know the value for the longer part? No, that is what we want to find. Label it with a question mark. We know the whole and one part.
     - How do we find the value of the missing part? We subtract.

2. Have students draw part-whole.
   - Have your students draw the models to solve **tasks 1-2, [US]p. 35 ([3d]p. 30)** in the textbook and write the equation needed.

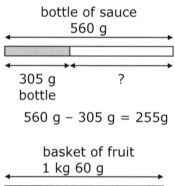

560 g – 305 g = 255g

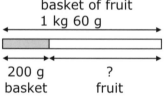

3. Discuss using comparison models to solve word problems.
   - Refer to **task 3, [US]p. 35 ([3d]p. 30)**.

1 kg 60 g – 200 g = 860 g

   - Tell your students that since we are comparing two people's weights, we can draw a separate bar for each weight. Both bars should be lined up at the left. Ask questions such as:
     - What information in the problem tells us the relative sizes of the two bars? One is three times as long as the other. Remind them that we show this as three parts the same size as the smaller bar, and that we can call each part a unit. When we draw models that have equal units, we will usually want to find the value of one of the units. If we know the value of more than one unit, we write that down as 3 units = 57 kg.
     - How do we find the value of one unit? We divide 57 kg by 3. Write 1 unit = 19 kg and point out that to go from 3 units to 1 unit we divide by 3, and to go from 57 kg to 19 g we do the same thing.

$$\div 3 \left(\begin{array}{l} 3 \text{ units} = 57 \text{ kg} \\ 1 \text{ unit } = 19 \text{ kg} \end{array} \right) \div 3$$

4. Discuss **tasks 4-9, [US]pp. 35-37 ([3d]pp. 30-32)**.

- You might want to call on a student to come up to the board and draw the model as you discuss it, without seeing the textbook.

5. Have students draw a model for **task 10, ^{US}p. 35-37 (^{3d}p. 32)**.
   - Students can work on this problem independently and then share their models and equations. Methods can vary. Discuss any alternate methods students might come up with. One possible model is given here.

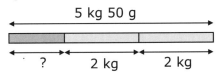

Workbook ^{US}Exercise 15 (^{3d}Exercise 16)

Activity 3.2b   **Practice**

2. Use **Practice 3B, ^{US}p. 38 (^{3d}p. 33)** to have students practice concepts learned in this unit.
   - Students can work individually or in groups and then share their solutions and models for the word problems. Possible models for #6 and #7 are shown here.
   - Discuss any alternate methods students may come up with for the word problems or in their models.
   - Provide additional review as needed. In particular, you may want to review some of the mental math from the first unit.

6.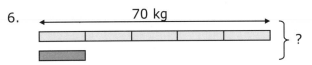

Son's weight = 70 kg ÷ 5 = 14 kg
Total weight = 70 kg + 14 kg = **84 kg**
   or: 14 kg x 6 = 84 kg

7.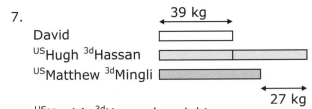

^{US}Hugh's ^{3d}Hassan's weight
   = 39 kg x 2 = 78 kg
^{US}Matthew's ^{3d}Mingli's weight
   = 78 kg – 27 kg = **51 kg**

US Part 3: Pounds and Ounces　　　　　　　　　　　　　　　　**4 sessions**

Objectives

- Review pounds and ounces.
- Estimate weight in pounds and ounces.
- Convert between pounds and ounces.
- Add and subtract pounds and ounces in compound units.

Materials

- Pound weights.
- Various ounce weights.
- Canned foods or other items that have the weight marked in pounds or ounces, or in ounces.
- Various weighing scales, including a balance scale.
- Objects that can be weighed.
- Pennies, paper clips.

Homework

- US Workbook Exercise 16

Notes

The standard units for weight used in the U.S., pounds and ounces, were introduced in *Primary Mathematics 2A*. Students weighed objects in either pounds or ounces. Here, students will read scales and weigh objects in pounds and ounces, and add and subtract pounds and ounces in compound units.

Students should have practical work in measuring weights using various weighing scales, if possible. Encourage them to estimate the weight before placing it on the scale. Estimation will give the students a better understanding of the units.

Remark, for teachers only: Pounds and ounces are a measure of weight (a measure of the force of gravity on an object), not of mass (a measure of the amount of matter in the object). (A "slug" is the U.S. unit of mass.)

On earth, 1 kg weighs 2.205 pounds or 35.28 ounces, and 1 ounce has a mass of 28.35 grams. You can tell your students that there are about 2 pounds in 1 kg. So a person who weighs about 80 pounds weighs about 40 kilograms.

A quart of water weighs about 2 pounds.

A slice of bread, about 60 paper clips, 11 pennies, or 5 quarters weigh about one ounce.

The abbreviation for pound, **lb**, comes from the Latin word *libra*, a unit of weight.

Activity 3.3a   **Pounds and Ounces**

1. Review pounds.
   - Show your students a 1-pound weight. Remind them that the pound is a unit of weight commonly used in the U.S. Most of the rest of the world now uses kilograms and grams, which are also used in science. But pounds and ounces are still used in the U.S. for everyday use.
   - Have them take turns handling the weight and feeling how heavy it is. You may also want to let them compare the pound weight to the kilogram weight.
   - Have students estimate the weight of various objects by feel as being about 1 lb, less than 1 lb, or more than 1 lb, and then weigh.

2. Review ounces.
   - Show your student various ounce weights. Remind them that the ounce is also a unit of weight. It is heavier than a gram. About 2 paper clips weigh a gram, but it would take about 56 paper clips to weigh about 1 ounce. 11 pennies weigh about 1 ounce, but 5 pennies weigh about 2 grams.
   - Have students take turns handling some ounce weights. You can also have them feel the weight of some objects marked in grams, such as canned food.
   - If you have enough balances and pennies, you can divide students into groups and have them find out how many ounces are in a pound.   **1 lb = 16 oz**

3. Read scales.
   - Refer to textbook, ^{US}**p. 39**.
     o Ask students to count the number of divisions between 0 lb and 1 lb. There are 16. Ask them for the value of each division. (1 oz)
     o Point out that only objects that weigh less than 1 lb can be weighed on the second scale.
     o Have students supply the answers for the two bottom scales.
   - Have students supply the answers for **task 1,** ^{US}**p. 40**.

4. Students estimate and weigh objects.
   - Divide students in groups.
   - Give each group some objects that weigh over 1 lb and have them estimate and then weigh them. Be sure that the scale or weighing machine the group is using can weigh the objects.
   - Students should record their measurements in a table.
   - Groups can exchange objects and measure the weight of each object.

Object	Weight	
	lb	oz
	lb	oz
	lb	oz

Activity 3.3b   **Convert between pounds and ounces**

1. Convert from pounds and ounces to ounces.
   Remind students that 1 lb = 16 oz. Discuss the   1 lb = 16 oz
   following or similar problems.

   - How many ounces are there in 2 lb?   1 lb = 16 oz x 1 = 16 oz
                                                            2 lb = 16 oz x 2 = 32 oz

   - In 3 lb?   3 lb = 16 oz x 3 = 48 oz

   - In 10 lb?   10 lb = 16 oz x 10 = 160 oz

   - In 3 lb 4 oz?   3 lb 4 oz = _____ oz
     o Find the number of oz in 3 lb, then add 4   3 lb 4 oz = 48 + 4 oz = 52 oz
       oz.

   - Have students supply the answer to, **task 2, ^{US}p. 40** in the textbook.
   - Use **Practice 3C, #1, ^{US}p. 42,** for additional problems.

2. Convert from ounces to pounds and ounces.
   Since division by a 2-digit number has not been taught yet, conversion from ounces to
   pounds will only involve small multiples of 16. Students can find the number of pounds by
   repeated subtraction, or by multiplying 16 by 1, 2, 3 or 4 to get the number of pounds.
   Discuss the process as follows or with similar questions.

   - How can we find the number of pounds in 48 oz?   48 oz = _____ lb
   - We can take away 16 oz for every pound.   48 oz
) – 16
                                                            32 oz
) – 16
                                                            16 oz
) – 16
                                                            0

                                                            48 oz = 3 lb

   - How about 39 oz?   39 oz = _____ lb

     o When we take away 32 oz for 2 pounds, we are   39 oz
       left with 7 oz.   ) – 16
                                                            23 oz
) – 16
                                                            7 oz

                                                            39 oz = 2 lb 7 oz

     o Or we can count up by 16 until we are going to   1 lb = 16 oz
       get more than the number of ounces there are   2 lb = 32 oz
       by adding another 16.   3 lb = 48 oz   too much
                                                            39 oz – 32 oz = 7 oz
                                                            39 oz = 2 lb 7 oz

- Have students supply the answer to **tasks 3-4, ^{US}p. 40** in the textbook. In task 4, it is probably easier to convert 6 lb 15 oz to ounces to compare, though some students may try to convert 115 oz to pounds and ounces.
- Use **Practice 3C, #3, ^{US}p. 42,** for additional problems.

3. Subtract ounces from 1 pound.
   - Give your students some ounces below 16 and ask them to tell you the number of ounces needed to make 1 pound. Write some subtraction equations for some of them. They need to find the difference from 16.

     1 lb – 11 oz = 5 oz
     1 lb – 6 oz = 10 oz

   - Write a problem such as 2 lb – 1 lb 6 oz where the difference is less than a pound. Lead them to see that they just need to "make 16" to bring the second number up to 2 lb.

     2 lb – 1 lb 6 oz = 10 oz

   - Provide additional problems for practice.

Activity 3.3c   **Add and subtract pounds and ounces in compound units**

1. Discuss strategies for adding ounces.
   - We can add the ounces and then convert to pounds and ounces.

     11 oz + 8 oz = 19 oz = 1 lb 3 oz
                              16 oz 3 oz

   - Or, we can make a 16 (1 pound), taking ounces from one of the numbers of ounces to make 16 with the other. The remainder is the number of ounces. In this example, we take 5 oz from the 8 oz to "make 16" with the 11 oz.

     11 oz + 8 oz = 1 lb 3 oz
         5 oz   3 oz

2. Discuss strategies for adding pounds and ounces.
   - Refer to **task 5(a), ^{US}p. 41** in the textbook.
   - We can add the pounds first, and then add the ounces using strategies already learned.

     3 lb 9 oz + 1 lb 14 oz

     3 lb 9 oz + 1 lb 14 oz = 4 lb 9 oz + 14 oz

     4 lb 9 oz + 14 oz   = 5 lb 7 oz
         7 oz 2 oz

   - Or, we can rewrite the problem vertically, add ounces, rename 16 oz as 1 lb, and add pounds.

     ```
           1
       3 lb   9 oz
     + 1 lb  14 oz   (9 oz + 14 oz = 23 oz = 1 lb 7 oz)
       5 lb   7 oz
     ```

3. Discuss strategies for subtracting ounces from pounds and ounces.

- We can rename one of the pounds as 16 ounces, add that to the 5 ounces, giving us 21 oz, and then subtract 9 oz from 21 oz to get 12 oz.
- Or, we can rename one of the pounds as 16 oz, subtract 9 oz from it, and add the difference to the remaining pounds and ounces.

$$3 \text{ lb } 5 \text{ oz} - 9 \text{ oz} = 2 \text{ lb } 21 \text{ oz} - 9 \text{ oz}$$
$$= 2 \text{ lb } 12 \text{ oz}$$

3 lb 5 oz – 9 oz = 2 lb 5 oz + 7 oz
= 2 lb 12 oz

2 lb 5 oz   1 lb

4. Discuss strategies for subtracting pounds and ounces.
- Refer to **task 5(b),** ^{US}**p. 41** in the textbook.
- We can subtract the pounds first, and then subtract the ounces using strategies we have already learned.

$$3 \text{ lb } 9 \text{ oz} - 1 \text{ lb } 14 \text{ oz} = 2 \text{ lb } 9 \text{ oz} - 14 \text{ oz}$$

2 lb 9 oz – 14 oz   = 1 lb 11 oz

1 lb 9 oz   1 lb

- Or, we can rewrite the problem vertically, rename 1 lb as 16 oz if necessary, subtract the ounces, and then subtract the pounds.

```
       2    25
      3 lb   9 oz
   -  1 lb  14 oz
      1 lb  11 oz
```

5. Use **Practice 3C, #3-6,** ^{US}**p. 42,** for additional problems. Students can work on the word problems individually or in small groups, and then share their methods and solutions. Discuss any alternate methods different students might have. One of the ways of solving #5 is given here.

5.

     3 oz   4 oz

Tomato

Avocado

Squash

Weight of avocado = 3 oz + 4 oz
= 7 oz
Weight of squash = 2 x 7 oz
= **14 oz**

Workbook ^{US}**Exercise 16**

Activity 3.3d **Practice**

1. Review this unit. You can use the worksheets on the next few pages and/or any problems from **Practices 1A-3C** not yet done. Answers to the worksheets are given below. Students can work on the word problems individually or in small groups, and then share their methods and solutions. Discuss any alternate methods different students might have.

Answers for Practice Set 4

1. (a) 64 oz   (b) 4 oz   (c) 68 oz

2. (a) 2 lb   (b) 2 lb 3 oz

3. (a) 10 lb 14 oz   (b) 11 lb 1 oz   (c) 14 lb 1 oz

4. (a) 10 oz   (b) 5 lb 0 oz
   (c) 4 lb 15 oz   (d) 3 lb 15 oz

5. (a) 134 oz   (b) 10 lb
   (c) 10 lb – 8 lb 6 oz = 1 lb 10 oz
   (d) 8 lb 6 oz + 6 lb 14 oz = 15 lb 4 oz

6. 15 oz + 15 oz = 1 lb 14 oz

Answers for Practice Set 5

1. (a) 7 lb 10 oz   (b) 2 lb 8 oz

2. (a) 48 oz   (b) 102 oz
   (c) 138 oz   (d) 82 oz
   (e) 1 lb 2 oz   (f) 2 lb 0 oz

3. 1 g, 1 oz, 1 lb, 1 kg

4. (a) 14 lb 1 oz   (b) 20 lb 0 oz   (c) 56 lb 3 oz
   (d) 6 lb 5 oz   (e) 21 lb 14 oz   (f) 1 lb 4 oz

5. Weight of smaller watermelon = 20 lb – 13 lb 9 oz = 6 lb 7 oz

6. Weight of the banana = 4 oz + 10 oz = 14 oz
   Weight of grapes = 14 oz + 14 oz + 14 oz = 1 lb 12 oz + 14 lb = 2 lb 10 oz

Answers for Practice Set 6

1. (a) 160 oz   (b) 127 oz   (c) 153 oz
   (d) 1 lb 8 oz   (e) 2 lb 1 oz

2. (a) 11 lb 4 oz   (b) 11 lb 6 oz
   (c) 5 lb 13 oz   (d) 12 lb 7 oz

3. (a) Total weight = 4 lb 8 oz + 2 lb 10 oz = 7 lb 2 oz
   (b) Difference in weight = 4 lb 8 oz – 2 lb 10 oz = 1 lb 14 oz

4. (a) Weight of cheese = 3 lb – 1 lb 12 oz = 1 lb 4 oz
       1 lb 4 oz = 20 oz
       Weight of 1 package of cheese = 20 oz ÷ 2 = 10 oz
   (b) 1 package cost $1
       Cost of 1 oz = $1 ÷ 10 = 100¢ ÷ 10 = 10¢

Practice Set 4

1. (a) 4 lb = _____ oz

   (b) 4 lb 4 oz = _____ oz more than 4 lb

   (c) 4 lb 4 oz = _____ oz

2. (a) 32 oz = _____ lb

   (b) 35 oz = _____ lb _____ oz

3. (a) 10 lb + 14 oz = _____ lb _____ oz

   (b) 10 lb 3 oz + 14 oz = _____ lb _____ oz

   (c) 10 lb 3 oz + 3 lb 14 oz = _____ lb _____ oz

4. (a) 1 lb − 6 oz = _____ oz

   (b) 5 lb 5 oz − 5 oz = _____ lb _____ oz

   (c) 5 lb 5 oz − 6 oz = _____ lb _____ oz

   (d) 5 lb 5 oz − 1 lb 6 oz = _____ lb _____ oz

5. (a) A pumpkin weighs 8 lb 6 oz. Write the weight in ounces.

   (b) A sack of potatoes weighs 160 oz. Write the weight in pounds.

   (c) How much heavier is the sack of potatoes than the pumpkin?

   (d) A banana squash weighs 6 lb 14 oz. What is the total weight of the pumpkin and the squash?

6. A can of soup weighs 15 oz. What the total weight of 2 cans of soup in pounds and ounces?

Practice Set 5

1. (a) 8 lb – 6 oz = _____ lb _____ oz

   (b) 3 lb – 8 oz = _____ lb _____ oz

2. Fill in the blanks.

   (a) 3 lb = _____ oz   (b) 6 lb 6 oz = _____ oz

   (c) 8 lb 10 oz = _____ oz   (d) 5 lb 2 oz = _____ oz

   (e) 18 oz = _____ lb _____ oz   (f) 32 oz = _____ lb _____ oz

3. Put in order from lightest to heaviest

   1 oz   1 g   1 kg   1 lb

4. Add or subtract in compound units.

   (a) 6 lb 12 oz + 7 lb 5 oz = _____ lb _____ oz

   (b) 12 lb 12 oz + 7 lb 4 oz = _____ lb _____ oz

   (c) 33 lb 8 oz + 22 lb 11 oz = _____ lb _____ oz

   (d) 10 lb 4 oz – 3 lb 15 oz = _____ lb _____ oz

   (e) 40 lb – 18 lb 2 oz = _____ lb _____ oz

   (f) 100 lb – 98 lb 12 oz = _____ lb _____ oz

5. The total weight of two watermelons is 20 lb. The larger watermelon weighs 13 lb 9 oz. What is the weight of the smaller watermelon?

6. An apple weighs 4 oz. A banana weighs 10 oz more than the apple. A bunch of grapes weighs three times as much as the banana. What is the weight of the grapes?

Practice Set 6

1. Fill in the blanks.

   (a) 10 lb = _____ oz

   (b) 7 lb 15 oz = _____ oz

   (c) 9 lb 9 oz = _____ oz

   (d) 24 oz = _____ lb _____ oz

   (e) 33 oz = _____ lb _____ oz

2. Add or subtract in compound units.

   (a)   10 lb 7 oz + 13 oz = _____ lb _____ oz

   (b)   4 lb 11 oz + 6 lb 11 oz = _____ lb_____ oz

   (c)   18 lb – 12 lb 3 oz = _____ lb_____ oz

   (d)   15 lb 12 oz – 3 lb 5 oz = _____ lb_____ oz

3. One squash weighs 4 lb 8 oz. Another squash weighs 2 lb 10 oz.
   (a)   What is the total weight of the two squashes?

   (b)   What is the difference in weight between the two squashes?

4. Two packages of cheese and a box of crackers together weigh 3 lb. The box of crackers alone weighs 1 lb 12 oz.

   (a)   How much does one package of cheese weigh?

   (b)   If Mary paid $2 for the two packages of cheese, what is the cost of 1 oz of cheese?

Review

Objectives
- Review all topics.

Suggested number of sessions: 2

	Objectives	Textbook	Workbook	Activities
Review				**2 sessions**
31	▪ Review.	^{US}pp. 43-44 ^{3d}pp. 34-35		R.1a
32				

Homework
- Workbook Review 1
- Workbook Review 2

Notes
Reviews in *Primary Mathematics* cover all previous material.

Activity R.1a

1. Have students work individually or in groups on the problems in **Review A and B, ^{US}pp. 43-44 (^{3d}pp. 34-35)** in the textbook and then have some share their solutions. One of the ways of solving #10 in Review A is given here.

2. Use any practice sets not yet done, mental math worksheets, or some games from previous units.

Review

Review A

10.

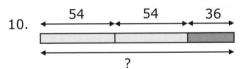

2 units = 2 x 54 = 108
Total oranges = 108 + 36 = **144**

or: Total oranges = 54 + 54 + 36 = 144

Unit 4 – Capacity

Objectives
- Review the liter.
- Understand the milliliter as a unit of capacity.
- Measure in liters and milliliters.
- Convert between liters and milliliters.
- Add or subtract liters and milliliters in compound units.
- [US]Review gallons, pints, quarts, and cups.
- [US]Convert between gallons, pints, quarts, and cups.
- [US]Add or subtract gallons, pints, quarts, and cups in compound units.

Suggested number of sessions: 7

	Objectives	Textbook	Workbook	Activities
Part 1 : Liters and Milliliters				**3 sessions**
33	• Review the liter. • Review the term capacity. • Understand the milliliter as a unit of measurement. • Estimate and measure capacity in liters and milliliters.	[US]pp. 45-48 [3d]pp. 36-39	Ex. 17 Ex. 18 Ex. 19	4.1a
34	• Convert between liters and milliliters. • Subtract milliliters from 1 liter.	[US]pp. 48-49, 51 [3d]pp. 39-50, 42 Practice 4A, #1-3	Ex. 20 Ex. 21	4.1b
35	• Add or subtract milliliters and liters in compound units. • Solve word problems involving capacity.	[US]pp. 50-52 [3d]pp. 41-43 Practice 4A, #4-5 Practice 4B	Ex. 22 [3d]Ex. 23	4.1c
[US]Part 2 : Gallons, Quarts, Pints and Cups				**4 sessions**
36	• Review gallons, quarts, pints, and cups. • Estimate and measure in gallons, quarts, pints, and cups. • Convert between gallons, quarts, pints, and cups	[US]pp. 53-54		4.2a 4.2b
37	• Convert from compound units to smaller units and vice versa. • Subtract cups from 1 pint, pints from 1 quart, and quarts from 1 gallon.	[US]pp. 54-56 [US]Practice 4C, #1-4		4.2c
38	• Add or subtract in compound units.	[US]p. 55 [US]Practice 4C, #5-8	[US]Ex. 23	4.2d
39	• Practice.			4.2e

Part 1: Liters and Milliliters **3 sessions**

Objectives

- Measure capacity in liters and milliliters.
- Estimate and compare capacities of containers.
- Convert between liters and milliliters.
- Add and subtract liters and milliliters in compound units.
- Solve word problems involving capacity.

Materials

- 1-liter beakers or measuring cups.
- 100-ml and 500-ml beakers.
- Teaspoon, medicine spoon marked in milliliters, or graduated cylinders.
- Various plastic containers of different shapes and sizes.
- Paper cups.
- Various empty commercial containers that have the capacity marked in liters and milliliters, such as detergent bottles.
- Pail, basin, etc.
- Water (use water colored with food coloring if possible since it is easier to see).

Homework

- Workbook Exercise 17
- Workbook Exercise 18
- Workbook Exercise 19
- Workbook Exercise 20
- Workbook Exercise 21
- Workbook Exercise 22
- [3d]Workbook Exercise 23

Notes

The standard unit, liter, was introduced in *Primary Mathematics 2A*. Here, students will learn about the milliliter as a standard unit, and measure capacity in liters and milliliters.

The capacity of a container is the amount of liquid it can hold. Students will not be using the term volume yet.

While students should be given practical experience in measuring capacity, this is difficult in a classroom situation. If your class does not have a sink, you could set up a workstation with tubs and containers and towels. Even so, to avoid spillage, you may have to do most of the actual pouring of liquids.

Students will also learn to add and subtract in compound units. Since $1 \ell = 1000$ ml, the process is the same as adding and subtracting kilometers and meters, or kilograms and grams.

Activity 4.1a   **Liters and milliliters**

1. Review liters.
   - Show your students a 1-liter beaker or measuring cup.
     - o Remind them that the liter is a standard unit of measurement.
     - o Fill the beaker with water to the 1-liter line.
     - o Tell students that the total amount of water in the beaker is 1 liter.
   - Show your students some containers filled with water.
     - o Tell them that the *capacity* of the container is the amount of liquid it can hold.
     - o Ask them to estimate the capacity as being less than, about, or greater than 1-liter.
     - o Place the beaker in a basin and pour water from the container into the beaker to determine if their estimate is correct.

2. Introduce milliliters.
   - Tell students that amounts of water less than 1 liter are measured in milliliters.
   - Show your student a teaspoon and tell them it holds about 5 milliliters of water. If you have medicine spoons or plastic 10-ml graduated cylinders you can have the students look at the markings on them.
   - Show student a centimeter cube. The unit cubes from base-10 blocks are centimeter cubes. Tell them that a container this size would have a capacity of 1 ml.
   - Show the students the liter beaker and draw their attention to the markings of milliliters. Have them determine the number of milliliters in a liter. You may have to call on a student to come up if you don't have enough beakers to pass around.   **1 ℓ = 1000 ml**
   - Show students the markings on 500-ml and 200-ml beakers, if you have some.
   - Pour water into the beakers and have students read the amount of water in milliliters. Make sure they understand the scale and the amount for each division.
   - Display some smaller containers that hold less than 1 liter. Fill them with water.
     - o Ask students to estimate the capacity of the containers.
     - o Pour the water into the beakers and let students see if their estimate is correct.

3. Measure in liters and milliliters.
   - Fill up a liter beaker and fill another liter beaker part way.
     - o Ask a student to come up and determine the amount of water in the second beaker. Then ask the class, "What is the total amount of water in the two beakers?"
     - o Write the amount down; for example, 1 ℓ 400 ml.
   - Discuss ^{US}**pp. 45-46 (^{3d}pp. 36-37)** in the textbook.
   - Discuss textbook, **tasks 3-4, ^{US}pp. 46-47 (^{3d}pp. 37-38)**.
   - Display some containers with the capacity marked in liters and milliliters and have the students read the capacity.
   - If possible, have students do **tasks 1, 2, and 5, ^{US}pp. 46, 48 (^{3d}pp. 37, 39)**.

4. Have students do **workbook exercises 17 and 18** in class.

Workbook Exercise 19

Activity 4.1b   **Convert between liters and milliliters**

1. Discuss converting between liters and milliliters.
   - Remind students that $1\,\ell = 1000$ ml.
     Write $1\,\ell = 1000$ ml on the board.
   - Discuss **tasks 6-11 and 13, ^{US}pp. 48-49 (^{3d}pp 39-40)** in the textbook.
   - Have students find the answers for **Practice 4A, problems 1-3, ^{US}p. 51 (^{3d}p. 42)**.

$$1\,\ell = 1000 \text{ ml}$$

$$700 \text{ ml} + 400 \text{ ml} = 1100 \text{ ml}$$

$$1100 \text{ ml} = 1\,\ell\,100 \text{ ml}$$
$$\swarrow \qquad \searrow$$
$$1000 \text{ ml} \qquad 100 \text{ ml}$$

$$2\,\ell\,5 \text{ ml} = 2005 \text{ ml}$$
$$\swarrow \qquad \searrow$$
$$2000 \text{ ml} \qquad 5 \text{ ml}$$

2. Discuss making $1\,\ell$ (1000) with milliliters.
   - Refer to **task 12, ^{US}p. 49 (^{3d}p 40)**.
   - Write the problem illustrated in this task as a missing number problem.
   - Students should see that, with the 650 ml, they need to make 1000.
   - You can rewrite the problem as a subtraction problem.
   - Provide some other problems where they need to bring the milliliters up to the next liter.

$$1\,\ell\,650 \text{ ml} + \underline{\hspace{2cm}} \text{ ml} = 2\,\ell$$

$$2\,\ell - 1\,\ell\,650 \text{ ml} = \underline{\hspace{2cm}}$$

$$3\,\ell - 2\,\ell\,5 \text{ ml} = \underline{\hspace{2cm}}$$

3. Have students do **workbook exercise 20** in class.

Workbook Exercise 21

Activity 4.1c   **Add or subtract milliliters and liters in compound units**

1. Add and subtract liters and milliliters in compound units.
   - Refer to **task 14, ^{US}p. 50 (^{3d}p 41)** in the textbook.
   - Discuss strategies for solving these problems. The same strategies that were used to add and subtract kilometers and meters or kilograms and grams apply here.
   - Use **Practice 4A, #4-5, ^{US}p. 42 (^{3d}p. 51)**, for additional problems.

2. Have students do **Practice 4B, ^{US}p. 52 (^{3d}p. 43)**.
   - Students can work individually or in groups and then share their solutions and models.
   - Discuss any alternate methods students may come up with for the word problems or in their models.

Workbook ^{US}Exercise 22 (^{3d}Exercises 22 and 23)

USPart 2: Gallons, Quarts, Pints and Cups   **3 sessions**

Objectives

- Review gallons, quarts, pints, and cups.
- Estimate and measure capacity in gallons, quarts, pints, and cups.
- Convert between gallons, quarts, pints, and cups.
- Add or subtract gallons, quarts, pints, and cups in compound units.

Materials

- Measuring cups with markings on the side, including a quart measuring cup.
- Various commercial items that are sold in gallons, quarts, pints and cups, such as diary products, particularly some gallon jugs, and including some half-gallon containers.
- Various plastic containers.
- Teaspoon, tablespoon.
- Basin or pail.
- Water, preferably colored.
- 4 sets of number cards 1-10 per group.
- Cards with "gallons", "quarts", "pints", and "cups" written on them, 6 of each per group.

Homework

- USWorkbook Exercise 23

Notes

The standard units for capacity used in the U.S., gallons, quarts, cups, and pints, were introduced in *Primary Mathematics 2A*. Here, students will learn to convert between these different units.

If possible, students should be given practical experience in measuring capacity. Cooking and baking are a familiar use for these units of capacity, so students might be given recipes to get practical experience with them.

The strategies already learned in converting between measurements and adding and subtracting compound measurements also apply here, except that the conversion factors are different.

A liter is almost equivalent to a quart.
1 liter = 1.057 quarts.
There are about 5 milliliters in a teaspoon, so a cup is about 240 ml.

2 c = 1 pt
2 pt = 1 qt
2 qt = 1 half-gallon
2 half-gallons = 1 gallon

4 c = 1 qt
4 qt = 1 gal

16 c = 1 gal

3 teaspoons = 1 tablespoon
4 tablespoons = ¼ cup
16 tablespoons = 1 cup

Activity 4.2a   **Gallons, quarts, pints, and cups**

1. Review gallons, quarts, pints, and cups.
   - Show your students a gallon jug, a half-gallon container, and some measuring cups. For the measuring cups, have them find the markings for cups and pints. (See textbook **task 1, ^{US}p. 53**)
   - Show students various containers and have them estimate their capacity in cups, pints, quarts, or gallons, depending on the size of the container. For smaller quantities, you could have students use water and measuring cups to determine if their estimate was close.
   - Compare a gallon to quart. Fill a liter beaker to the line, and then pour into a quart measuring cup. Your quart measuring cup may have markings in both liters and milliliters. You can point out that a cup is about 250 milliliters.

2. Convert between gallons, quarts, pints, and cups.
   - If you can, have students work in groups to determine the number of cups in a pint, pints in a quart, quarts in a half-gallon, and half-gallons in a gallon. Or, you can demonstrate, using water and containers. Write the results on the board.

      2 c = 1 pt
      2 pt = 1 qt
      2 qt = 1 half-gallon
      2 half-gallons = 1 gallon

   - Guide them in determining the number of cups in a quart, quarts in a gallon, and cups in a gallon. You can use a diagram:

      4 c = 1 qt
      4 qt = 1 gal

      cup
      pint
      quart
      half-gallon
      gallon

      16 c = 1 gal

   - Discuss textbook **task 2, ^{US}p. 54**.
   - Ask some additional questions such as the following, which require students to convert between gallons, quarts, pints, and cups such as the following. Guide them in determining the relevant conversion factor (2, 4, or 16) and whether the problem involves multiplication (e.g. from gallons to quarts) or division (e.g. from quarts to gallons. Draw diagrams with units. Students can also convert in steps (e.g. halve to go from cups to pints to quarts to half-gallons to gallons or double to go in the other direction).
      o A carton of orange juice holds 1 pint. How many cups is this?
      o A carton of milk holds 1 quart. How many pints is this? How many cups?
      o The capacity of a milk jug is 1 gallon, which is 4 quarts. What is the capacity of the jug in cups?
      o 1 qt = _____ pt
      o 4 pt = _____ c
      o 8 c = _____ qt

      8 cups
      8 cups = 4 pints = 2 quarts
      or:
      8 cups ÷ 4 = 2 quarts

Activity 4.2b　　　　　　　**Convert between gallons, quarts, pints, and cups**
Group activity

Material for each group of four:
- 4 sets of number cards 1-10.
- Cards with "gallons", "quarts", "pints", and "cups" written on them, 6 of each giving a total of 24 "capacity cards".

Procedure
- Shuffle the number cards and deal all out. Cards are kept in a stack face-down in front of each student.
- Shuffle the capacity cards and place them face down in a pile in the middle.
- Each student turns over one number card from his stack and two unit cards from the middle.
- The student must convert the number from the largest volume unit to the smallest. For example, the student turns over a "4" from his stack, and a "cup" and a "quart" from the stack in the middle. The quart is a larger capacity than the cup. So the student must answer the problem 4 qt = _____ c. The student records the play as 4 qt = 16 c.
- If both capacities are the same, no conversion is necessary. A student could record 10 c = 10 c if he or she turned over a "10", a "cup", and another "cup".
- The measurement cards are placed in a discard pile face up.
- The play continues until all number cards have been turned over. If there are less than 4 players in a group, the measurement cards in the discard pile will have to be reshuffled and placed face-down again in the middle.

Activity 4.2c　　　　　　　　　**Convert compound units**

1. Convert into compound units.
   - Refer to **task 3, ^{US}p. 54** in the textbook.
     - We add the quarts together. Since we know that there are 4 quarts in a gallon, we can convert the 5 quarts into 1 gallon and 1 quart.
     - Point out that if we divide 5 by 4, the answer is 1 with a remainder of 1. The quotient is the number of gallons, and the remainder the number of quarts. (Students have done division with a remainder in *Primary Mathematics 3A*.)
     - Point out that we can also add by making a 4 as shown, since we know that will make a gallon. That leaves 1 qt.

   3 qt + 2 qt = 5 qt
   　　　　　　　= 1 gal 1 qt

   3 qt + 2 qt = 1 gal 1 qt
   　　1 qt　1 qt

   - Refer to textbook, **task 4, ^{US}p. 54**.
     - To find the number of gallons, we need to find how many fours are in 78, since there are 4 quarts in a gallon. We can divide 78 by 4. The quotient is the number of gallons, and the remainder the number of quarts left over. We are finding the number of fours (gallons) in 78 quarts.
     - We can also divide by 2 to get the number of half-gallons, and then by 2 again to get the number of quarts.

   78 ÷ 4 = 19 r 2
   78 qt = 19 gal 2 qt

- Refer to textbook, **task 5, [US]p. 55**.
  - o This time, we are finding the number of quarts in 15 pints. Since 2 pints are in a quart, we need to divide by 2 to find the number of twos in 15. The remainder is the number of pints left over.

$$15 \div 2 = 7\ r\ 1$$
$$15\ pt = 7\ qt\ 1\ pt$$

- Have students solve **tasks 5-7, [US]p. 55.**

2. Convert from compound units.
   - Discuss some problems where we need to convert from a compound unit to the smaller unit, such as the following.
     - o 5 pt 1 c = 11 c
       - ▪ Find the number of cups in 5 pints and then add the remaining 1 cup.
       - ▪ Since there are 2 cups in a pint, we multiply the number of pints by 2.

$$1\ pt = 2\ c$$
$$5\ pt\ 1\ c = \underline{\hspace{2cm}}$$
$$5\ pt = 5 \times 2\ c = 10\ c$$
$$10\ c + 1\ c = 11\ c$$

   - o 2 gal 3 qt = 11 qt
     - ▪ Multiply the gallons by 4 to get the number of quarts in 2 gallons, and add the quarts.

$$1\ gal = 4\ qt$$
$$2\ gal\ 3\ qt = \underline{\hspace{2cm}}$$
$$2\ gal = 2 \times 4\ qt = 8\ qt$$
$$2\ gal\ 3\ qt = 8\ qt + 3\ qt = 11\ qt$$

- Use **Practice 4C, #1-4, [US]p. 56,** for additional problems. Students can solve them individually and then share their answers.

Activity 4.2d   Add and subtract gallons, quarts, pints, and cups in compound units

1. Discuss addition of compound units.
   - Refer to **task 8, [US]p. 55** in the textbook.
     - o Add the pints first, then the cups.
     - o Convert cups to pints.

$$2\ pt\ 1\ c + 3\ pt\ 1\ c$$
$$2\ pt\ 1\ c \xrightarrow{\ +\ 3\ pt\ } 5\ pt\ 1\ c$$
$$5\ pt\ 1\ c \xrightarrow{\ +\ 1\ c\ } 5\ pt\ 2\ c = 6\ pt$$

   - Discuss another problem with a larger conversion factor, such as 4 gal 2 qt + 3 gal 3 qt.
     - o Add the gallons first.
     - o Add the quarts.
       - ▪ We can find the total quarts and convert to gallons and quarts and add that.
       - ▪ Or, we can get our answer by making a gallon with the 2 quarts.

$$4\ gal\ 2\ qt + 3\ gal\ 3\ qt$$
$$4\ gal\ 2\ qt + 3\ gal\ 3\ qt = 7\ gal\ 2\ qt + 3\ qt$$
$$7\ gal\ 2\ qt + 3\ qt = 7\ gal\ 5\ qt$$
$$= 8\ gal\ 1\ qt$$
$$7\ gal\ 2\ qt + 3\ qt = 8\ gal\ 1\ qt$$
$$2\ qt \quad 1\ qt$$

2. Discuss subtraction of compound units.
   - Discuss a problem such as   7 gal 2 qt – 3 gal 3 qt
     7 gal 2 qt – 3 gal 3 qt
     - Subtract the gallons first.   7 gal 2 qt – 3 gal 3 qt = 4 gal 2 qt – 3 qt
     - Subtract the quarts.
       - We can rename 1 gal 2 qt as 6 qt   4 gal 2 qt – 3 qt = 3 gal 6 qt – 3 qt
         and then subtract.   = 3 gal 3 qt
       - Or, we can subtract the quarts
         from one of the gallons.   4 gal 2 qt – 3 qt = 3 gal 3 qt
                                         3 gal 2 qt   1 gal

   - Use **Practice 4C, #5-8, US p. 56,** for additional problems. Students can solve them individually and then share their answers. Students can draw models for #6-8.

Workbook US Exercise 23

Activity 4.2e   **Practice**

1. Use the worksheets on the next few pages and/or any problems from **Practices 4A-4C** not yet done. Answers to the worksheets are given below. Students can work on the word problems individually or in small groups, and then share their methods and solutions. Discuss any alternate methods different students might have.

2. You can use the Practice Set 9 to review conversion factors.

Answers for Practice Set 7

1. (a) <   (b) <   (c) >   (d) =
2. 1 qt, 4 pt 1 c, 1 gal 2 c, 20 c
3. (a) 19 pt 0 c   (b) 22 gal 2 qt
   (c) 1 gal 2 qt   (d) 20 qt 1 c
4. (a) Total capacity = 15 gal 2 qt + 14 gal 3 qt = 30 gal 1 qt
   (b) Difference = 15 gal 2 qt – 14 gal 3 qt = 3 qt
5. Capacity in gallons = 84 ÷ 4 = 21 gal

Answers to Practice Set 8

1. (a) 20   (b) 17
   (c) 14   (d) 25
   (e) 48   (f) 22
2. (a) <   (b) >   (c) =
3. (a) 14 qt 0 pt   (b) 85 gal 2 qt   (c) 24 pt 1 c
4. Amount of milk left = 6 gal – 3 gal 1 qt = 2 gal 3 qt
5. Total milk = 2 c x 14 = 28 c = 7 qt
6. Water needed = 1 gal – 1 pt = 4 qt – 1 pt = 8 pt – 1 pt = 7 pt

Answers to Practice Set 9

1. 8	2. 36	3. 4	4. 5000	5. 6000	6. 8
7. 32	8. 36	9. 24	10. 8	11. 4000	12. 100
13. 8000	14. 6000	15. 700	16. 3000	17. 27	18. 20
19. 600	20. 16	21. 3000	22. 24	23. 4000	24. 160
25. 40	26. 18	27. 8000	28. 700	29. 32	30. 84

Practice Set 7

1. Put >, <, or = in the circles.

   (a) 3 pt $\bigcirc$ 7 c   (b) 8 pt 1 c $\bigcirc$ 18 c

   (c) 33 c $\bigcirc$ 2 gal   (d) 30 qt $\bigcirc$ 7 gal 2 qt

2. Put in order from smallest amount to largest amount

   4 pt 1 c   20 c   1 gal 2 c   1 qt

3. Add or subtract in compound units

   (a) 12 pt 1 c + 6 pt 1 c = _____ pt _____ c

   (b) 12 gal 3 qt + 9 gal 3 qt = _____ gal _____ qt

   (c) 10 gal 1 qt – 8 gal 3 qt = _____ gal _____ qt

   (d) 36 qt – 15 qt 3 c = _____ qt _____ c

4. One fish tank has a capacity of 15 gal 2 qt.
   The second fish tank has a capacity of 14 gal 3 qt.

   (a) What is the total capacity of the two fish tanks?

   (b) What is the difference in capacity of the two fish tanks?

5. The capacity of a tank is 84 qt. How many gallons of water can it hold?

Practice Set 8

1. Fill in the blanks.

   (a) 10 pt = _____ c   (b) 8 pt 1 c = _____ c

   (c) 7 qt = _____ pt   (d) 12 qt 1 pt = _____ pt

   (e) 12 gal = _____ qt   (f) 5 gal 2 qt = _____ qt

2. Fill in the circle with >, =, or <

   (a) 5 gal 2 qt ◯ 23 qt

   (b) 22 qt 1 pt ◯ 40 pt

   (c) 6 qt 1 c ◯ 25 c

3. Add or subtract.

   (a) 10 qt 1 pt + 3 qt 1 pt = _____ qt _____ pt

   (b) 100 gal 1 qt – 14 gal 3 qt = _____ gal _____ qt

   (c) 301 pt – 276 pt 1 c = _____ pt _____ c

4. Mr. Jones bought 6 gallons of milk for his 4 teenage boys. They drank 3 gal 1 qt in 3 days. How much milk was left?

5. Devon drinks 2 cups of milk daily. How many quarts of milk does he drink in 2 weeks?

6. The capacity of a jug is 1 gal. There is one pint of water in it now. How many more pints of water are needed to fill it up?

Practice Set 9

1. 4 qt = _____ pt

2. 9 gal = _____ qt

3. 2 pt = _____ c

4. 5 ℓ = _____ ml

5. 6 km = _____ m

6. 1 gal = _____ pt

7. 2 lb = _____ oz

8. 3 ft = _____ in.

9. 8 yd = _____ ft

10. 2 qt = _____ c

11. 4 kg = _____ g

12. 1 m = _____ cm

13. 8 km = _____ m

14. 6 ℓ = _____ ml

15. 7 m = _____ cm

16. 3 km = _____ m

17. 9 yd = _____ ft

18. 5 qt = _____ c

19. 6 m = _____ cm

20. 1 lb = _____ oz

21. 3 kg = _____ g

22. 2 ft = _____ in.

23. 4 ℓ = _____ ml

24. 10 lb = _____ oz

25. 5 gal = _____ pt

26. 6 yd = _____ ft

27. 8 kg = _____ g

28. 7 m = _____ cm

29. 2 gal = _____ c

30. 7 ft = _____ in.

Unit 5 – Graphs

Objectives
- Relate bar graphs to picture graphs with scales.
- Read and interpret bar graphs.
- Solve problems using information from bar graphs

Suggested number of sessions: 3
(Student understanding may benefit by stretching the activities into 4 or 5 sessions.)

	Objectives	Textbook	Workbook	Activities
Part 1 : Bar Graphs				**3 sessions**
40	• Relate bar graphs to picture graphs with scales. • Read scales on bar graphs. • Read and interpret bar graphs.	^{US}pp. 58-59 ^{3d}pp. 45-46	Ex. 24, #1-2	5.1a
41	• Read and interpret bar graphs.	^{US}pp. 60-61 ^{3d}pp. 47-48	Ex. 24, #3 Ex. 25, #1-2	5.1b
42	• Read and interpret bar graphs.	^{US}pp. 62-63 ^{3d}pp. 49-50	Ex. 25. #3	5.1c

Part 1: Bar Graphs (^{US}pp. 58-63, ^{3d}pp. 45-50) **3 sessions**

Objectives

- Relate bar graphs to picture graphs with scales.
- Read and interpret bar graphs.
- Solve problems using information from bar graphs

Materials

- Prepared graph paper (see activity 5.1a).
- Colored chalk in 5 or more colors.
- Several sets of crayons in 5 or more colors.
- Illustrations of bar graphs from magazines or newspapers.

Homework

- Workbook Exercise 24
- Workbook Exercise 25

Notes

Students learned to read and interpret picture graphs with scales (1 picture standing for 2, 3, 4, or 5 items) in *Primary Mathematics 2B*.

Here, they will learn to read and interpret bar graphs.

Students should be able to interpret bar graphs in both horizontal and vertical forms.

Students will learn to construct bar graphs *in Primary Mathematics 4*.

Activity 5.1a   **Relate bar graphs to picture graphs with scales**

1. Discuss the picture graph on [US]p. 58 ([3d]p. 45) in the textbook. Point out that each € stands for 2 fish.
   - Ask a student, "How many fish were caught by [US]Matthew ([3d]Minghua)?" Ask the class, "How many agree with that answer?" If there is an error, discuss.
   - Continue with the other questions in the same manner. How many fish were caught by each of the other boys?

2. Collect data and construct a picture graph.
   - On the board, list 5 colors such as red, blue, green, purple, and orange. Ask students to choose their favorite color.
   - Keep track of their choices with tally marks. Total the tally marks for each color and write the totals on the board.
   - Draw a picture graph to represent the results. Each square represents two students. Ask students what to do if an odd number of students chose a particular color. Use half a square for the odd number.

3. Refer to [US]p. 59 ([3d]p. 46) in the textbook.
   - Compare the bar graph with the picture graph on the previous page and discuss how the scaling of the bar graph is represented.
   - Have students supply the answers to the questions about the bar graph.

4. Have students construct a bar graph from the picture graph on the board.
   - Provide students with crayons and graph paper, with the scale already marked on the left, such as the one on p. 94 of this guide, and lead them in constructing a bar graph from the picture graph. Or, form students into groups to work together on this bar graph.
   - Instructions to students:
     o The bars should be separated by a space.
     o Mark the color represented under each bar.
   - Discuss the data in the graph, using questions similar to those in the text.

5. Collect data and construct another bar graph.
   - On the board, list 5 food items such as pancakes, waffles, muffins, donuts, brownies. Ask students to choose their favorite.
   - Keep track of their choices with tally marks. Total the tally marks for each item and write the totals on the board.
   - Provide students with crayons and graph paper, with the scale already marked on the left, and lead them in constructing a bar graph from the picture graph. Or, form students into groups to work together on this bar graph.
   - Discuss the data in the graphs

Workbook Exercise 24, problems 1 and 2

Activity 5.1b   **Read and interpret bar graphs**

1. Discuss the bar graph in **task 1, [US]p. 60 ([3d]p. 47)** in the textbook.
   - Have students first notice the scale. Each division has a value of 10.
   - Have students supply the answers to the questions about the graph.

2. Construct another bar graph with divisions in 5's.
   - Provide students with data where there are up to 100 of each item, such as the number of students in grades 1 to 5 in a school. For simplicity, the data amounts should be multiples of 5.
   - Give students graph paper with divisions marked on the left, in 5's.
   - Guide them in drawing in the bars and in marking each bar correctly.
   - Discuss the graphs they made. Ask question such as, "Which class has the most students?" "How many more students are in grade 4 than in grade 3?"

3. Discuss the bar graph **task 2, p. ^{us}61 (3^dp. 48)** in the textbook
   - Have students supply the answers to the questions about the graph.

4. Construct a horizontal bar graph, with the same data used for the graph above, or with new data.
   - Give students graph paper with divisions marked on the bottom, in 5's.
   - Guide them in drawing in horizontal bars and marking each bar on the left.
   - Discuss the graphs they made. Make sure students understand that both horizontal and vertical bar graphs give exactly the same information.

Workbook Exercise 24, problem 3 and Exercise 25, problems 1 and 2

Activity 5.1c   **Read and interpret bar graphs**

1. Discuss the graph in **task 3, ^{us}p. 62 (^{3d}p. 49)** in the textbook.
   - Have students determine the **vertical** scale.
     - o Point out that only every second mark is labeled as 10s. Ask, what does each mark measure? (5)
     - o Have students supply the answers to the textbook's questions for the graph.

2. Discuss the graph in the textbook, **task 4, ^{us}p. 63 (^{3d}p. 50)**.
   - Have students determine the **vertical** scale.
   - Point out that the scale is marked off in 10s, with labels every 5th mark.
   - Discuss the difference in scale between the p. 62 and p. 63 graphs.
   - Explain that scales are chosen to be appropriate for the data the graph is to represent.
   - Have students supply the answers to the text's questions for the graph.

3. Have students open their workbooks to **Exercise 25, problem 3**. Discuss the bar graph.
   - Point out the dashed lines from the scale to the tops of the bars to the scale on the left.
   - Have students supply the answers to the questions about the graph.

4. Provide additional bar graphs from science or social studies texts, or magazines or newspapers. Make sure to include one or more horizontal graphs.
   - Discuss the scales and have students both pose and answer questions from the graphs. Discuss the information the writers are trying to convey to readers using the graphs. Give students one or more such bar graphs to paste into their journals.
   - For homework, they should study the graphs and write down as many facts as they can, from the bar graphs.

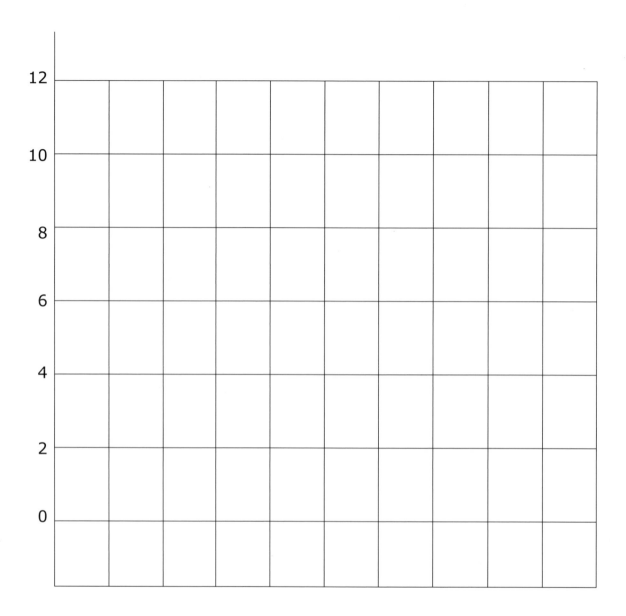

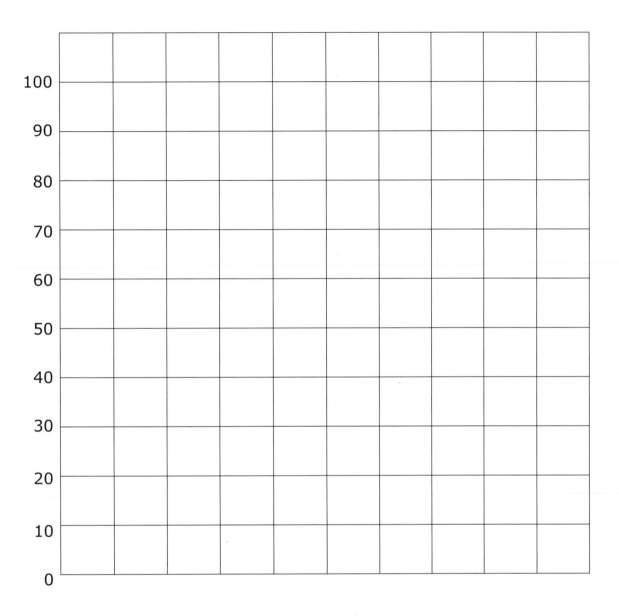

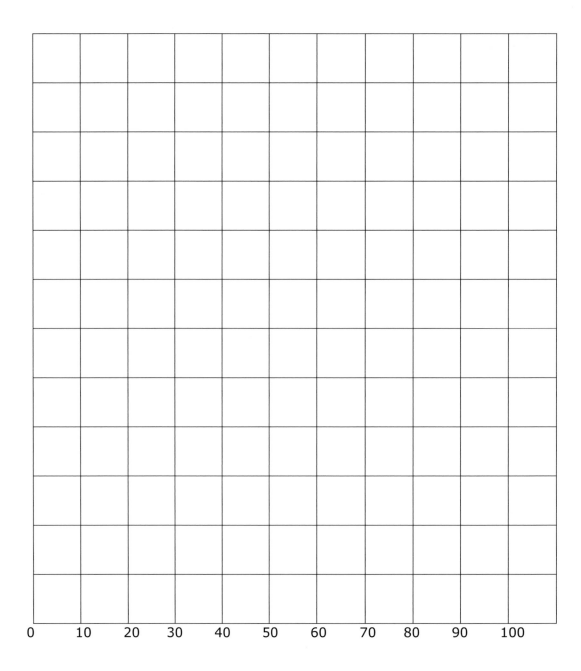

0   10   20   30   40   50   60   70   80   90   100

Review

Objectives
- Review all topics.

Suggested number of sessions: 2

	Objectives	Textbook	Workbook	Activities
Review				**2 sessions**
43	▪ Review topics from Primary	^{US}p. 57	Review 3	R.2a
44	Mathematics.	^{3d}p. 44	Review 4	

Homework

- Workbook Review 3
- Workbook Review 4

Activity R.2a **Review**

1. Have students work individually or in groups on the problems in **Review C**, ^{US}**p. 57** (^{3d}**p. 44**) in the textbook and then have some share their solutions.

2. Include in the review any practice sets not yet done, mental math worksheets, or some games from previous units.

3. You can include some of the problems from the homework in class.

Unit 6 – Fractions

Objectives

- Recognize and name fractions of a whole.
- Visualize relative sizes of fractions of a whole.
- Understand the terms numerator and denominator.
- Compare and order fractions with a common numerator.
- Compare and order fractions with a common denominator.
- Recognize and name equivalent fractions for fractions with denominators up to 12
- Find equivalent fractions.
- Find the simplest form of a fraction.
- Compare and order fractions.

Suggested number of sessions: 9

	Objectives	Textbook	Workbook	Activities
Part 1 : Fractions of a Whole				**3 sessions**
45	▪ Recognize and name fractions of a whole. ▪ Make a whole with a fraction.	^{US}pp. 64-66 ^{3d}pp. 51-53	Ex. 26 Ex. 27 Ex. 28	6.1a
46	▪ Understand the terms numerator and denominator. ▪ Compare and order fractions with a common numerator. ▪ Compare and order fractions with a common denominator.	^{US}pp. 67-68 ^{3d}pp. 54-55	Ex. 29	6.1b
47	▪ Practice	^{US}pp. 69 ^{3d}pp. 56	Ex. 30	6.1c 6.1d
Part 2 : Equivalent Fractions				**6 sessions**
48	▪ Recognize and name equivalent fractions. ▪ Find equivalent fractions using fraction bars.	^{US}pp. 70-71 ^{3d}pp. 57-58	Ex. 31	6.2a
49	▪ Find equivalent fractions using multiplication.	^{US}pp. 72 ^{3d}pp. 59	Ex. 32	6.2b
50	▪ Find equivalent fractions using division.	^{US}pp. 73 ^{3d}pp. 60	Ex. 33	6.2c 6.2d 6.2e
51	▪ Find the simplest form of a fraction.	^{US}pp. 73-74 ^{3d}pp. 60-61	Ex. 34	6.2f
52	▪ Compare and order simple fractions	^{US}pp. 74 ^{3d}pp. 61	Ex. 35	6.2g
53	▪ Practice	^{US}pp. 75 ^{3d}pp. 62		6.2h 6.2i

Part 1: Fractions of a Whole (^{US}pp. 64-69, ^{3d}pp. 51-56)   **3 sessions**

Objectives

- Recognize and name fractions of a whole.
- Make a whole with a fraction.
- Understand the terms numerator and denominator.
- Visualize relative sizes of fractions of a whole.
- Compare and order unit fractions.
- Understand the terms numerator and denominator.
- Compare and order fractions with a common numerator.
- Compare and order fractions with a common denominator.

Materials

- Fraction circles and bars.
- Fraction cards – see activities 6.1b and 6.1d.
- Number cards 1-12, four sets per group.
- Number cube with 1-6.
- Copies of fraction bars sheet.

Homework

- Workbook Exercise 26
- Workbook Exercise 27
- Workbook Exercise 28
- Workbook Exercise 29
- Workbook Exercise 30

Notes

In *Primary Mathematics 2B* the student learned to understand and write fractional notation, to find sums of fractions that make a whole, and to order unit fractions. This is reviewed in this section. The terms **numerator** and **denominator** are introduced here, and students will learn how to compare and order fractions with a common numerator or denominator.

For many students, the imposing terms *numerator* and *denominator* hinder understanding. These terms have to be learned, but some students are better able to focus on the mathematics when the informal terms **top** and **bottom** are used instead in classroom conversations. So when you do have to use the terms *numerator* and *denominator*, make sure you also display an illustration such as shown here on the board. *Numerator* and *denominator* will be introduced in later grades. For now, emphasize *top* and *bottom*.

The denominator gives the number of equal parts the whole is divided into. The numerator gives the number of equal parts represented by the fraction.

The denominator also indicates the size of the part; the larger the denominator the smaller the size since the whole is divided up into more parts.

$\frac{3}{5}$ and $\frac{3}{8}$ have the same number of parts, but the parts for $\frac{3}{8}$ are smaller. So $\frac{3}{8}$ is smaller than $\frac{3}{5}$. $\frac{3}{5}$ and $\frac{2}{5}$ have the same size parts, but $\frac{2}{5}$ has fewer parts, so $\frac{2}{5}$ is smaller than $\frac{3}{5}$.

$$\frac{3}{8} < \frac{3}{5}$$
$$\frac{2}{5} < \frac{3}{5}$$

Students learned the meaning of the *is less than* and *is greater than* symbols in *Primary Mathematics 2A*. If you use them, you may need to remind students that the pointed end points to the smaller number.

Activity 6.1a   **Fractions of a whole**

1. Review fractions.

   • Write a fraction on the board, such as $\frac{1}{4}$, and ask your students to draw a picture to show what this means. They may draw any shape, such as a square, rectangle, or a circle, and divide that into four equal parts.

   • Discuss ^{US}p. 64 (^{3d}p. 51) in the textbook.

   • Discuss everyday use of fractions, such as sharing cookies, eating a fifth of a pizza, quarters of a dollar, sharing half your room with your brother, etc. Restrict the discussion to fractions of a 1 whole, rather than a fraction of a quantity (such as a fourth of $20).

   • Discuss **task 3**, ^{US}p. 64 (^{3d}p. 51) in the textbook in detail. Ask students to call out the answers for each figure.
     o "What fraction of each shape is shaded?"
     o "What fraction of each shape is NOT shaded?"

   • Draw a diagram illustrating $\frac{3}{4}$ on the board, such as a circle divided into fourths. Color three parts.
     o Ask students what fraction of the circle is colored.
     o Lead students to see that $\frac{3}{4} = \frac{1}{4} + \frac{1}{4} + \frac{1}{4}$.
     o Ask them what part is uncolored, then write that on the board: $\frac{1}{4}$. Remind students that $\frac{1}{4}$ can be read as "one fourth" or "one quarter".
     o Ask them how many fourths make a whole. Lead them to see that 1 whole = $\frac{4}{4}$ = 4 fourths.
     o Lead them to see, and write on the board, that "1 fourth and 3 fourths together make 4 fourths, or one whole. $\frac{1}{4} + \frac{3}{4} = \frac{4}{4}$ = 1.

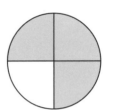

$$\frac{3}{4} = \frac{1}{4} + \frac{1}{4} + \frac{1}{4}$$

$$1 = \frac{4}{4}$$

$$1 = \frac{1}{4} + \frac{3}{4}$$

   • Draw a large fraction bar, such as one showing fifths. Ask questions such as:
     o The bar is one whole. How many parts are there?
     o What fraction of the whole bar is one part?
     o What fraction is shaded?
     o How many parts is that?
     o What fraction is not shaded?
     o What is the total if we add the shaded fraction to the unshaded fraction?
     o What is the sum of the two numbers on the top of the fractions?

$$\frac{3}{5} = \frac{1}{5} + \frac{1}{5} + \frac{1}{5}$$

$$\frac{2}{5} = \frac{1}{5} + \frac{1}{5}$$

$$\frac{3}{5} + \frac{2}{5} = \frac{5}{5} = 1$$

3. Discuss **tasks 1-2**, ^{US}p. 65 (^{3d}p. 52). Then go over as much as you can of Exercises 26-28 with the class, and assign the rest as homework.

Workbook Exercises 26-28

Activity 6.1b   **Compare and order fractions**

1. Discuss the terms *numerator* (*top*) and *denominator* (*bottom*).
   - Draw on the board a large fraction bar, divided into sevenths.
   - Tell students that the number on the **top** is called the **numerator**
   - Tell students that the number on the **bottom** is called the **denominator**.
   - Lead them to see that the bottom number (the denominator) tells us the number of parts the whole is divided into. The more parts the bar is divided into, the smaller each part will be.
   - Lead them to see that the top number (the numerator) tells us how many parts the fraction has.
   - Write $\dfrac{3}{7} + \dfrac{4}{7} = 1$

   - Point out that in $\dfrac{3}{7} + \dfrac{5}{7} = 1$ the bottom numbers are the same, and the top numbers add to the same number as the bottom number.

   - Is the following true? $\dfrac{3}{7} + \dfrac{5}{6} = 1$ Why not?

   - Is the following true? $\dfrac{3}{6} + \dfrac{2}{6} = 1$ Why not? Illustrate with a fraction bar. Make the total length of the fraction bar the same as the fraction bar for sevenths on the board.

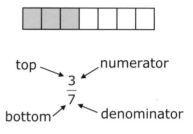

$$\frac{3}{7} + \frac{4}{7} = 1$$

2. Discuss **task 4, ^{US}p. 67 (^{3d}p. 54)** in the textbook.

3. Order unit fractions.
   - Ask a student who likes pizza whether they would want a fourth of a pizza or a fifth. Why?
   - Use fraction circles.
     - o Show three thirds, then set aside one third. Show two halves, then set aside a half. Do the same with fifths and fourths. Have students name the fractions you set aside.
     - o Write the fractions. Ask students to put them in order from smallest to largest.
     - o Remove the fraction circle pieces. Ask them how they could tell which was smaller if they did not have a picture.
     - o The fraction with the largest denominator is the smallest fraction. Ask them why. It is the smallest piece.

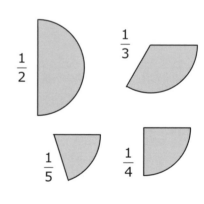

$$\frac{1}{5} < \frac{1}{4} < \frac{1}{3} < \frac{1}{2}$$

4. Compare fractions with the same numerator.
   - Draw or display a fraction bar for fifths under one for thirds. Give students copies of the fraction pars which have their unit fraction markings filled in (see the next page).

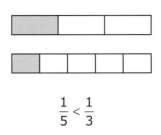

   - Ask students to mark or color the leftmost $\frac{1}{3}$ and $\frac{1}{5}$ parts on their own bars. Do the same on the board. Ask whether $\frac{1}{3}$ or $\frac{1}{5}$ is smaller.

$$\frac{1}{5} < \frac{1}{3}$$

   - Remind students that the bottom number tells us how many parts are in the whole. When the whole is divided into five parts, each part is one fifth. When the whole is divided into 3 parts, each part is one third. So the larger bottom of $\frac{1}{5}$ means the fraction is a smaller part of the whole than the smaller bottom of $\frac{1}{3}$.

   - Ask students whether $\frac{2}{3}$ or $\frac{2}{5}$ is smaller. Have them mark or color those second units on their bars. Do the same on the board.

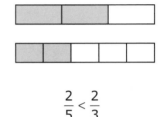

   - Remind them that $\frac{2}{5} = \frac{1}{5} + \frac{1}{5}$ and $\frac{2}{3} = \frac{1}{3} + \frac{1}{3}$, and we already know that $\frac{1}{5}$ is smaller than $\frac{1}{3}$.

$$\frac{2}{5} < \frac{2}{3}$$

   - Do a few other examples comparing fractions with the same numerator (greater than 1) but different denominators.

5. Compare fractions with the same denominator.
   - Have students use their sheet of paper with fraction bars and mark or color $\frac{3}{8}$ and $\frac{5}{8}$. Write the fractions on the board.

$$\frac{3}{8} < \frac{5}{8}$$

   - Ask them which is larger.
   - Lead them to see that the denominators are the same, so the parts are the same size, but the numerators are different, and the one with the larger numerator is the larger fraction since it has more parts.

6. Discuss **tasks 5-10, USpp. 67-68 (3dpp. 54-55)** in the textbook.
   - For task 10, allow students to use the sheet with fraction bars, if necessary. You can give them new sheets so they can color the fractions they are comparing.
   - Ask students to order the fractions $\frac{3}{5}$, $\frac{3}{7}$, and $\frac{4}{5}$ and explain their reasoning. $\frac{3}{7}$ is less than $\frac{3}{5}$ (same numerator, larger denominator) and $\frac{4}{5}$ is greater than $\frac{3}{5}$, so the order from smallest to largest is $\frac{3}{7}$, $\frac{3}{5}$, $\frac{4}{5}$.

Workbook Exercise 29

A fraction bar diagram. The top bar represents 1. Successive rows divide the whole into equal parts:
- $\frac{1}{2}$, $\frac{1}{2}$
- $\frac{1}{3}$, $\frac{1}{3}$, $\frac{1}{3}$
- $\frac{1}{4}$, $\frac{1}{4}$, $\frac{1}{4}$, $\frac{1}{4}$
- $\frac{1}{5}$ (×5)
- $\frac{1}{6}$ (×6)
- $\frac{1}{7}$ (×7)
- $\frac{1}{8}$ (×8)
- $\frac{1}{9}$ (×9)
- $\frac{1}{10}$ (×10)
- $\frac{1}{11}$ (×11)
- $\frac{1}{12}$ (×12)

Activity 6.1c **Review fractions**

1. Use **Practice 6A, ^{US}p. 69 (^{3d}p. 56)** in the textbook to review this section. You can also have students play the game in the next activity.

2. Compare and order fractions.
   - Divide students into groups.
   - Give each group a set of around 8 fraction cards to arrange in order. The fraction cards can be any fraction up to $\frac{11}{12}$. Or, instead of fraction cards, give students a list of fractions which they must rewrite in
     - ascending order
     - descending order.
   - Students can use their fraction bar sheets to put them in order.
   - Some can be arranged according to common numerator and denominator.
   - Groups can share their results with the class.

Workbook Exercise 30

Activity 6.1d **Make a whole**
Game

Material for each group of about 4 students:
- Fraction cards:

$$\frac{1}{2}, \frac{1}{2}, \frac{1}{3}, \frac{2}{3}, \frac{1}{4}, \frac{2}{4}, \frac{2}{4}, \frac{3}{4}, \frac{1}{5}, \frac{2}{5}, \frac{3}{5}, \frac{4}{5}, \frac{1}{6}, \frac{2}{6}, \frac{3}{6}, \frac{3}{6}, \frac{4}{6}, \frac{5}{6},$$

$$\frac{1}{7}, \frac{2}{7}, \frac{3}{7}, \frac{4}{7}, \frac{5}{7}, \frac{6}{7}, \frac{1}{8}, \frac{2}{8}, \frac{3}{8}, \frac{4}{8}, \frac{4}{8}, \frac{5}{8}, \frac{6}{8}, \frac{7}{8}, \frac{1}{9}, \frac{2}{9}, \frac{3}{9}, \frac{4}{9},$$

$$\frac{5}{9}, \frac{6}{9}, \frac{7}{9}, \frac{8}{9}, \frac{1}{10}, \frac{2}{10}, \frac{3}{10}, \frac{4}{10}, \frac{5}{10}, \frac{5}{10}, \frac{6}{10}, \frac{7}{10}, \frac{8}{10}, \frac{9}{10}$$

Procedure:
- Shuffle the cards and place face down.
- Place the top two cards face up on the table.
- Players take turns drawing cards. If the player can match his card to a card on the table (with the same denominator) to make a whole, the player keeps both cards. (Both cards must have the same denominator, i.e. they cannot match $\frac{1}{2}$ with $\frac{4}{8}$ even though that does make a whole.) If not, the card is placed face up on the table.
- Play continues until all cards have been turned over.

| Part 2: Equivalent Fractions (^{US}pp. 70-77, ^{3d}pp. 57-64) | 6 sessions |

Objectives

- Recognize and name equivalent fractions for fractions with denominators up to 12.
- Find equivalent fractions.
- Find the simplest form of a fraction.
- Compare and order fractions.

Materials

- Strips of paper, 4 for each student. Cut strips the length of a sheet of paper.
- Fraction circles and bars.
- Fraction cards – see activity 6.2e.

Homework

- Workbook Exercise 31
- Workbook Exercise 32
- Workbook Exercise 33
- Workbook Exercise 34
- Workbook Exercise 35

Notes

The concept of equivalent fractions is introduced here. $\frac{1}{2}$, $\frac{2}{4}$, $\frac{3}{6}$, and $\frac{4}{8}$ are all equivalent fractions; they all name the same part of the whole. Later, students will be adding and subtracting fractions with different denominators, which cannot be done without the use of equivalent fractions. Fraction bars and circles will be used to understand equivalent fractions.

We can change a fraction into an equivalent fraction by <u>multiplying</u> both the numerator and denominator by the same number.

$$\overset{\times 3}{\frac{2}{3}} = \frac{6}{9} \underset{\times 3}{}$$

We can also change a fraction into an equivalent fraction by <u>dividing</u> both the numerator and denominator by the same number.

$$\overset{\div 3}{\frac{6}{9}} = \frac{2}{3} \underset{\div 3}{}$$

A fraction can be <u>simplified</u> when its numerator and denominator can be divided by the same number. $\frac{6}{9}$ can be simplified to the equivalent fraction $\frac{2}{3}$ by dividing both the numerator and denominator by 3. If it is not possible to divide both the numerator and denominator by any number except 1, the fraction is said to be in its simplest form. $\frac{2}{3}$ is a fraction in its simplest form. The numerator and denominator do not have a common factor.

Students will work with equivalent fractions in several ways. Equivalent fractions are important in comparing fractions. For example, to compare $\frac{4}{5}$ and $\frac{7}{10}$ they make use of being able to multiply both the numerator and denominator of $\frac{4}{5}$ by two to get the equivalent fraction $\frac{8}{10}$. Then they can compare $\frac{8}{10}$ with $\frac{7}{10}$. This lets them see that $\frac{4}{5}$ is greater than $\frac{7}{10}$.

Comparing fractions with denominators that are not simple multiples of each other, such as $\frac{2}{5}$ and $\frac{1}{3}$, takes more care. Students will list equivalent fractions for both fractions to find fractions of each that have the same denominator.

$$\frac{2}{5}: \frac{4}{10}, \frac{6}{15}$$

$$\frac{1}{3}: \frac{2}{6}, \frac{3}{9}, \frac{4}{15}$$

They can then compare $\frac{6}{15}$ and $\frac{4}{15}$ to determine that $\frac{2}{5}$ is greater than $\frac{1}{3}$. Note that they are essentially finding a common multiple of 5 and 3. Some students may see that they can start with the fraction with the larger denominator, $\frac{2}{5}$, until they get one with a denominator that is a multiple of the smaller denominator, $\frac{1}{3}$, and then find the equivalent fraction of $\frac{1}{3}$ with a denominator of 15 without listing all the other equivalent fractions.

Activity 6.2a   **Equivalent fractions**

1. Discuss equivalent fractions using fraction bars. Give each student four strips of paper. You can use the following discussion:
   - Set two of the strips down in front of you.
   - How many parts does each strip have? (1)
   - We have one part out of 1, and we can write it as $\frac{1}{1}$.
   - Fold one piece in half. Unfold and draw a line where the fold was.
   - How many parts does this bar have? (2)
   - What fraction is each part? (one half)
   - How many halves are there in one whole? (2)   How many parts do we need to have a whole? (2)
   - We need 2 parts out of 2. We can write it as $\frac{2}{2}$.
   - Is $\frac{1}{1}$ equal to $\frac{2}{2}$? (Yes)
   - For the second strip, we have twice as many parts, but each part is half as big.
   - Fold a third piece in half, and half again and then unfold and draw lines where the folds were. (Demonstrate).
   - How big is each part? (one fourth)
   - How many fourths are there in a whole? (4)
   - Color half of the strip showing halves, and half of the strip showing fourths.
   - What is the fraction that is colored in each strip?
   - ($\frac{1}{2}$ and $\frac{2}{4}$) Is $\frac{1}{2}$ equal to $\frac{2}{4}$? (Yes)
   - Fractions like $\frac{1}{2}$ and $\frac{2}{4}$, which have different numerators (tops) and denominators (bottoms) but are equal, have a special name. These equal fractions are called **equivalent fractions**.
   - Fold another piece in half, half again, and half again and mark the folds as before.
   - How big is each part? (one eighth)
   - How many eighths are there in a whole? (8)
   - Color the first four parts.
   - What fraction is colored? (Write on the board $\frac{4}{8}$ and four eighths.)
   - Are $\frac{2}{4}$ and $\frac{4}{8}$ equivalent fractions? (Yes)
   - What are some other equivalent fractions for $\frac{1}{2}$? ($\frac{5}{10}$, $\frac{6}{12}$ ...)

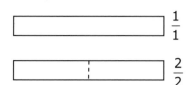

$$\frac{1}{1} = \frac{2}{2}$$

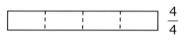

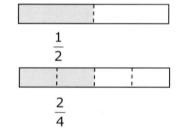

$$\frac{1}{2} = \frac{2}{4}$$

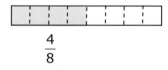

4 eighths

$$\frac{2}{4} = \frac{4}{8}$$

2. Discuss equivalent fractions using fraction circles.
   - Display or draw a circle on the board. Show thirds. Color in two thirds.
   - Ask students to tell you what fraction this is of the circle.
   - Draw the same diagram, and then split each third in half. Ask students for the fraction that is shaded.
   - Ask them if $\frac{2}{3}$ and $\frac{4}{6}$ are the same.
   - Ask them what they are called. (Equivalent fractions)
   - You can continue to divide the parts to show the equivalent fraction $\frac{8}{12}$.

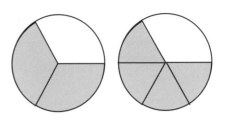

$$\frac{2}{3} = \frac{4}{6}$$

3. Go over ^{US}pp. 70-71 (^{3d}pp. 57-58) in the textbook with the class. Go over each step, or choose a student to read and explain each step to the class. Then discuss **task 1, ^{US}p. 71 (^{3d}p. 58)**.

4. Give students copies of the labeled fraction bars. You may want them to cut apart the bars so they can compare them more easily.
   - Get students to name other equivalent fractions.
   - Write some equivalent fractions with a missing numerator for the second fraction and get students to use their fraction bars to find the number that goes in the numerator.

$$\frac{5}{6} = \frac{\square}{12}$$

Workbook Exercise 31

Activity 6.2b   **Find equivalent fractions using multiplication**

1. Ask students if they have discovered an easy way to find equivalent fractions when they don't have fraction strips to look out. Allow students to share their ideas.

2. Remind students of the paper strips they folded in the previous activity. Draw the fraction bars on the board.
   - Ask students how many parts there are total for the bar showing halves. Ask the same thing for the bar showing fourths. The total number of parts double.
   - How about the total number of shaded parts? They double also.
   - Each part is now half as big, so twice as many are needed to have an equal amount of the whole shaded.
   - When the number of shaded parts is doubled, the total number of parts is also doubled, or multiplied by 2.
   - Ask student how many parts there are total for the bar showing eighths, and how many parts are shaded.
   - How does this compare to the bar showing halves?
   - When the number of shaded parts is multiplied by 4, the total number of parts is also multiplied by 4.

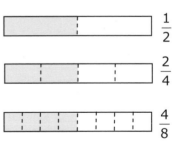

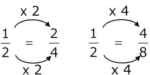

3. Refer to **task 1, ᵁˢp. 71 (³ᵈp. 58)** in the textbook.
   - Ask students to determine what number the first denominator was multiplied by to get the second denominator. For example, in (a), 3 is multiplied by 2 (3 x 2 = 6).
   - Have them multiply the numerator by the same number. They should see that they get the equivalent fraction that is shown in the fraction bars.

4. Discuss **tasks 2-3, ᵁˢp. 72 (³ᵈp. 50)** in the textbook.
   - For task 3, have students also give you the number that they multiply the numerator and denominator by to find the missing numbers.

Workbook Exercise 32

Activity 6.2c   **Find equivalent fractions using division**

1. Draw fraction bars for eighths and halves, shading in one half on both. Write $\frac{4}{8} = \frac{1}{2}$.

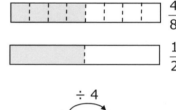

   - Ask students if they see a way of getting from $\frac{4}{8}$ to the equivalent fraction $\frac{1}{2}$. They may suggest division.

   - Point out that the total number of parts is divided by 4. The number of shaded parts is also divided by 4.
   - We can find an equivalent fraction by dividing the fraction's top (numerator) and bottom (denominator) by the same number.

2. Discuss **task 4, ᵁˢp. 73, ³ᵈp. 60** in the textbook.
   - You can illustrate this on the board as well with a rectangle. Tell students it is easier to see and count small parts such as $\frac{8}{12}$ with a rectangle.

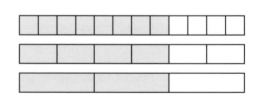

   - Illustrate some other problems, such as $\frac{8}{10} = \frac{\square}{5}$ with rectangles. Point out that we must first determine what 10 is divided by to get to 5, and then divide the numerator by the same number.

3. Have students supply the answers for **task 5, ᵁˢp. 73, ³ᵈp. 60** in the textbook.
   - Have them also you the number they used to divide both the numerator and denominator.

4. Give students four numbers and have them make up two equivalent fractions using the four numbers.

                                                 4, 10, 8, 5

   $$\frac{\square}{\square} = \frac{\square}{\square}$$

Homework: Workbook Exercise 33

Activity 6.2d   **Common factors review**
Game

To find equivalent fractions using division, such as finding the simplest form of a fraction (activity 6.2f) students need to be able to determine when two numbers can be divided by the same number (common factors). At this level they only need to be able to do this for numbers 1-12. You can give them a list of fractions and have them find a number by which both the numerator and denominator can be divided. Or you can have the students review this with a game.

Material for each group of 3-4 students:
- Four or more sets of number cards 1-12.
- Number cube marked with 1-6.

Procedure:
- Shuffle the cards and place face down in the middle.
- Turn over five cards and place them face up on the table.
- The players take turns throwing the number cube and getting as many multiples of the number on the number cube as possible (cards with numbers that can be divided by the number rolled). For example, there are cards for 1, 5, 6, 8 and 12 in the center. The player throws a 4. He can remove the cards 8 and 12. Note that if he throws a 1, he gets all the cards in the center.
- After each turn, replace the cards that have been removed with more cards from the stack.
- Play continues until all cards have been removed.

Activity 6.2e   **Identify equivalent fractions**
Game

Material for each group of students:
- 66 fraction cards for $\frac{1}{2}$ through $\frac{12}{12}$, e.g. $\frac{1}{2}$, $\frac{2}{2}$, $\frac{1}{3}$, $\frac{2}{3}$, $\frac{3}{3}$, etc.

Procedure:
- Shuffle cards and place face down. Turn over top card.
- Students take turns turning over the next card. If it is an equivalent fraction for any card on the table the student keeps both cards.
- Play continues until all cards are used up.

Activity 6.2f   **Simplest form**

1. Find simplest form.
   Refer to **task 6, ^{US}p. 73 (^{3d}p. 60)** in the textbook.

   - Have students find equivalent fractions for $\frac{6}{12}$.

   $$\frac{6}{12} = \frac{3}{6} = \frac{1}{2}$$

   - Have them see if they can find equivalent fractions for each of those by using division.

   $$\frac{6}{12} = \frac{2}{4} = \frac{1}{2}$$

   - Point out that with each division, both the top of the fraction (numerator) and bottom (denominator) get smaller.

   $$\frac{6}{12} = \frac{1}{2}$$

   - Tell them that $\frac{1}{2}$ is an equivalent fraction that is in the simplest form.
     - Simplest form is a term we use when there is no number that can divide both the top (numerator) and bottom (denominator) of a fraction. (If a student points out that we can divide both the top and bottom by 1, show him that the fraction will stay the same.) There is no common factor for the top and bottom other than 1.

   - Have them divide both the top and bottom of $\frac{8}{12}$ by 2.

     Then, since both the top and bottom of $\frac{4}{6}$ can be divided by 2, have them divide again.

   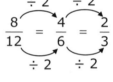

   - Point out we could also have divided the top and bottom of $\frac{8}{12}$ by 4.

   - As long as both the numerator and denominator can still be divided by the same number, the fraction is not in simplest form.

2. Identify fractions in their simplest form.
   - Give students some fractions and have them tell you if the fraction is in simplest form.
   - See if they can find any patterns. Any fraction with an even number in both the numerator and denominator is not in simplest form. They can try first dividing both the numerator and denominator by 2, then by 3, then by 5. They can also try 4 or 6.
   - You may want to try a few fractions with a denominator greater than 12.

3. Students supply the answers for **task 7 ^{US}p. 74, (^{3d}p. 61)**.

4. Write fractions in simplest form.
   - Write 5 numbers between 1 and 12 on the board   2, 3, 5, 8, 9
     - Have students make as many fractions in their simplest form as they can.
     - This activity can also be done in groups. Give each $\frac{2}{3}, \frac{3}{5}, \frac{8}{9}$, etc
       group a set of 5 numbers. Have a representative of each group write their fractions on the board.

Workbook Exercise 34

Activity 6.2g **Compare and order fractions**

1. Compare related fractions (one denominator is a simple multiple of the other).
   - Provide students with the sheet of fraction bars.
   - Have them compare two fractions, such as $\frac{3}{4}$ and $\frac{5}{8}$.

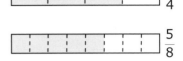

   $\frac{5}{8}$ is smaller than $\frac{3}{4}$.
   - Ask them how we can compare the two fractions without fraction bars or pictures.
     - We need fractions with the same bottom (denominator) so we can compare them.
   - Ask students to find the equivalent fraction for $\frac{3}{4}$ with a denominator of 8. It is $\frac{6}{8}$. Since $\frac{5}{8}$ is less than $\frac{6}{8}$, $\frac{5}{8}$ is smaller than the fraction $\frac{3}{4}$.

$$\frac{3}{4} = \frac{6}{8}$$
$$\frac{5}{8} < \frac{6}{8}$$
$$\text{so } \frac{5}{8} < \frac{3}{4}$$

   - Discuss **tasks 8-9, ^{US}p. 74, (^{3d}p. 61)** in the textbook.

2. Compare simple unrelated fractions (one denominator is a not a simple multiple of the other). Note: This concept can be difficult for your students. Have them compare unrelated fractions with fraction bars. Comparing unrelated fractions will be revisited in *Primary Mathematics 4*.
   - Ask students which is greater, $\frac{1}{3}$ or $\frac{2}{5}$.
     - Here, the denominator 3 cannot be multiplied by a number to get an equivalent fraction with a 5 as the denominator.
     - We can list equivalent fraction for both $\frac{1}{3}$ and $\frac{2}{5}$ until we get fractions with the same denominator.
     - For this, we multiply both the top (numerator) and bottom (denominator) of each fraction by 2, then by 3, and so on until we get to two with the same denominator.

$$\frac{2}{5}, \frac{4}{10}, \left(\frac{6}{15}\right)$$
$$\frac{1}{3}, \frac{2}{6}, \frac{3}{9}, \frac{4}{12}, \left(\frac{5}{15}\right)$$

3. Students supply the answers for **tasks 10-12, ^{US}p. 74 (^{3d}p. 61)**.

4. (Optional) Write the following fractions and ask your student if each of them is greater than or less than $\frac{1}{2}$, and why:
   - $\frac{3}{8}$ less; $\frac{4}{8}$ is equivalent to $\frac{1}{2}$, and $\frac{3}{8}$ is less than $\frac{4}{8}$. 3 is less than half of 8.
   - $\frac{5}{6}$ more; $\frac{3}{6}$ is equivalent to $\frac{1}{2}$; $\frac{5}{6}$ is more than $\frac{3}{6}$. 5 is more than half of 6.
   - $\frac{7}{12}$ more; 7 is more than half of 12.

- $\dfrac{4}{10}$ less; 4 is less than half of 10.

- $\dfrac{5}{7}$ more; half of 7 is more than 3 but less than 4, which is half of 8. So 5 is more than half of 7.

- $\dfrac{2}{5}$ less; 2 is less than half of 5.

Workbook Exercise 35

Activity 6.2h   **Review equivalent fractions**

1. Use **Practice 6B, ^{US}p. 75, ^{3d}p. 62** to review this section.

2. Students can play any of the games from this unit, or do activity 6.2i.

Activity 6.2i   **Order fractions**
Group activity

Material for each group of students:

- 66 fraction cards for $\dfrac{1}{2}$ through $\dfrac{12}{12}$, e.g. $\dfrac{1}{2}$, $\dfrac{2}{2}$, $\dfrac{1}{3}$, $\dfrac{2}{3}$, $\dfrac{3}{3}$, etc.

Procedure:
- Shuffle cards an place face down.
- Each student draws five cards and arranges the fractions in increasing order. If fractions are equivalent they are placed on top of each other.
- The group can also work together. First they draw 2 cards and arrange them in order. Then they draw 3 cards and arrange them in a new line. Then they draw 4 cards and arrange them in order, and so on.

Review

Objectives
- Review all topics.

Suggested number of sessions: 2

	Objectives	Textbook	Workbook	Activities
Review				**2 sessions**
54	▪ Review topics from Primary Mathematics.	^{US}pp. 76-77 ^{3dp}p. 63-64	Review 5	R.3a
55			Review 6	

Homework

- Workbook Review 5
- Workbook Review 6

Activity R.3a   **Review**

1. Review
   - Have students work individually or in groups on the problems in **Review D**, ^{US}**pp. 76-77** (^{3d}**pp. 63-64**) in the textbook and then have some share their solutions.
   - Include in the review any practice sets not yet done, mental math worksheets, or some games from this or previous units.

Unit 7 – Time

Objectives

- Tell time to the 1 minute interval.
- Use a.m. and p.m.
- Find the duration of time intervals when given the start and end times.
- Find start or end time when given the duration and the end or start time.
- Convert between hours, minutes, and seconds, between years and months, and between weeks and days.
- Add or subtract hours and minutes in compound units.

Suggested number of sessions: 10

	Objectives	Textbook	Workbook	Activities
Part 1 : Hours and Minutes				**6 sessions**
56	• Review a.m. and p.m. • Understand the relative magnitudes of hours and minutes. • Tell time to 1-minute intervals.	^{US}p. 79 ^{3d}p. 66	Ex. 36	7.1a
57	• Find the duration of a time interval using a clock face.	^{US}p. 78, pp. 80-81 ^{3d}p. 65, pp. 67-68	Ex. 37	7.1b
58	• Convert hours and minutes to minutes and vice versa.	^{US}p. 82 ^{3d}p. 69	Ex. 38	7.1c 7.1d
59	• Find the duration of a time interval without using a clock face. • Find the end time when given the start time and the time interval. • Find the start time when given the end time and the time interval.	^{US}p. 83 ^{3d}p. 70	Ex.39	7.1e
60	• Add or subtract time in compound units.	^{US}pp. 84-85 ^{3d}pp. 71-72	Ex. 40	7.1f
61	• Solve problems involving time.	^{US}p. 86 ^{3d}p. 73		7.1h
Part 2 : Other Units of Time				**4 sessions**
62	• Understand the second as a unit of measurement. • Measure time in seconds. • Convert from minutes and seconds to seconds and vice versa.	^{US}pp. 87-88 ^{3d}pp. 74-75	Ex. 41 Ex. 42	7.2a
63	• Understand the calendar. • Learn the months of the year. • Convert between years and months in compound units.	^{US}pp. 88 ^{3d}pp. 75	Ex. 43	7.2c
64	• Learn the days of the week. • Convert between weeks and days in compound units.	^{US}pp. 88 ^{3d}pp. 75	Ex. 44	7.2d 7.2e
65	• Review. • Solve problems involving time.	^{US}pp. 88 ^{3d}pp. 75		7.2g

Part 1: Hours and Minutes (^{US}pp. 78-86, ^{3d}pp. 65-73)   **6 sessions**

Objectives

- Tell time to the 1-minute interval.
- Understand and use a.m. and p.m. in telling time.
- Convert between hours and minutes.
- Find the duration of a time interval.
- Find the end time when given the start time and the duration.
- Find the start time when given the end time and duration.
- Add and subtract time in compound units.

Materials

- Large demonstration clock.
- Geared clocks for students.
- Stopwatch.
- Pairs of cards with hours and minutes on one and corresponding minutes on the other. A set of 10 to 20 pairs per group.

Homework

- Workbook Exercise 36
- Workbook Exercise 37
- Workbook Exercise 38
- Workbook Exercise 39
- Workbook Exercise 40

Notes

In *Primary Mathematics 2B* students learned to tell time to the 5-minute interval and to use a.m. and p.m. They also learned to find the duration of time intervals or start or end times using a clock face.

Now, students will learn to tell time to the 1-minute interval, to solve problems involving time intervals without as well as with a clock face, and to add and subtract time in compound units.

To help students learn how to solve problems involving duration, a time line is introduced. Time lines can be marked in various ways; with the hours like a number line, or hour to hour as we count up the hours to find the duration of the time interval. Time lines seem to be especially helpful with subtraction: finding the start time when given the end time and the duration. Students are not required to — but can — draw timelines; they are more of a teaching tool for you.

We can convert hours and minutes to minutes and vice versa using strategies similar to those used with other measurements, except that here the conversion factor is 60.

We can add in compound units by "making 60" to get to the next hour.

$$2 \text{ h } 45 \text{ min} + 30 \text{ min} = 3 \text{ h } 15 \text{ min}$$
$$15 \text{ min} \quad 15 \text{ min}$$

We can subtract in compound units by subtracting the minutes from one of the hours (60 minutes) if there are not enough minutes.

$$2 \text{ h } 15 \text{ min} - 45 \text{ min} = 1 \text{ h } 15 \text{ min} + 15 \text{ min}$$
$$= 1 \text{ h } 30 \text{ min}$$
$$1 \text{ h } 15 \text{ min} \quad 60 \text{ min}$$

Activity 7.1a   **Time to 1-minute intervals**

1. Review the clock face.
   - Provide students with some geared clock faces.
   - Display a demonstration clock and have student observe the simultaneous movement of the minute and hour hands.
   - Let the students experiment with their own clocks.
   - Remind students that the numbers mark the hours. The shorter hand points to the hours, the longer one marks the minutes and makes one full turn for each hour. The smaller marks are for minutes.
     - Ask students how many minutes are between each number on the clock. (5)
     - Have students count by 5's as you move the minute hand from number to number. They see that 1 hr = 60 min.

2. Discuss the relative magnitude of hours and minutes.
   - Have students tell you some events that take about an hour or about a half hour. List these on the board.
   - Use a stopwatch and have students do some activity for 1 minute, such as that given in the **task 1, ^{US}p. 79 (^{3d}p. 66)** in the textbook, or trying to hop on one foot for a minute. Since some student's names are longer than others, they won't write their names the same number of times. The point is to get an idea of how long a minute is.
   - You may want to discuss ways in which time is subjective. For example, the minute seemed very long when they were doing an activity that was timed, but if they were not paying much attention to the time, or doing something fun, a minute could seem to last for a much shorter time. An hour seems to go by fast when playing, but could seem to go by much more slowly in math class!

3. Review ways to talk about time, a.m. and p.m., and telling time to 5-minute intervals.
   - You may want to begin by reminding them that long before clocks, sun dials were used to keep track of time. Since the sun is highest in the sky at noon, time was named before noon and after noon. Now, we still say a time is either a.m. (from "ante-meridian" which means "before noon" in Latin) or p.m. (from "post-meridian, which means "after noon").
   - Pick some activity, such as waking up in the morning, and ask a student what time he or she wakes up. Show the time on the clock.
   - Write the time in digital notation, as in 6:45 a.m.
   - Remind students that a.m. means the time in the morning.
   - Have students give different ways of talking about the time, such as
     - six forty-five a.m.
     - a quarter to seven in the morning. (Show that the hand has moved three quarters of the way around.)
   - Continue with other activities throughout the day, going to p.m. times and pointing out why we need p.m. (there are two sets of 12 hours in the day).
   - You can also discuss military time, and time based on 24 hours. Many countries use 24 hours, rather than 12.
   - Have the students set some of the times on their clocks. Give the time various ways, such as "a quarter past one" or "twenty to six."
   - Tell them that you do an activity at a certain time, show the time on your clock, and have them tell you what time it is.

4. Have students supply the answers for **task 2, ^{US}p. 79 (^{3d}p. 66)** in the textbook

5. Tell time to the 1-minute interval.
   - Set the demonstration clock for 4:43. Ask students to tell you the time. Write the time. Discuss ways of finding the time.
     o We can count by fives to 4:40, and then by ones to 4:43.
     o By now, some of the students may be able to recognize 4:40, and only have to count up from that.
     o Or they can count up from 4:30 by fives to 4:40, then by ones to 4:43.
     o Ask them how many minutes it is to 5:00.
   - Do a few other examples.
   - Have students work in pairs and take turns. One student sets a time, the other writes the time. Or, one student writes a time, the other shows it on their clock.

Workbook Exercise 36

Activity 7.1b   **Time duration**

1. Find the duration of time intervals for minutes and hours.
   - Use a demonstration clock. Provide students with geared mini-clocks.
   - Discuss ^{US}**p. 78** (^{3d}**p. 65**) in the textbook. Students can move the minute hand from the start to the end time and count the minutes by 5's.
   - Have students do **task 3, ^{US}p. 80 (^{3d}p. 67)**. Students can use their clocks.
   - Have students do **task 4, ^{US}p. 80 (^{3d}p. 67)**. Point out that the hour hand in the second example is just before the 7, and then moves to just before the 8. It moves 5 divisions, or what would be 5 minutes for the minute hand.
   - Have students set a time, such as 2:33, and have them find the time 4 hours later by moving the minute hand only. They should see that as the minute hand goes completely around for each hour, the hour hand moves to the same relative spot between the numbers, but at the next interval.
   - Write a time, such as 8:30 a.m., and have the student find the time for 6 hours later, where the hour goes from a.m. to p.m., using their clocks and moving the minute hand around as they count the hours. They should note that they have gone from before 12:00 to after 12:00.

2. Find the duration of time intervals for both hours and minutes.
   - Provide students with geared clocks.
   - Have students do **task 5, ^{US}p. 81 (^{3d}p. 68)**.
   - Point out that in the last example, the hour hand starts out a bit past 9, and ends up a bit past 11. 2 hours have passed. The minute hand is 15 minutes beyond where it would be if just hours have passed. So hours and minutes have passed.
   - Use task 5(c) to introduce a time line. Draw a line and mark 9:15 on it. At regular intervals, mark 10:15 and then 11:15. The next interval would be 12:15, which is past the end time of 11:30, so stop at 11:15. Then make another mark a bit past 11:15 for 11:30 and show the distance as 15 min.

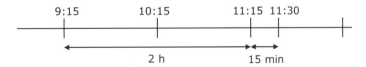

- Provide some other examples. Include one or two examples that go from a.m. to p.m. (They will need to do this in Exercise 37, #2.(d). If time is running short, do not spend too much time on discussions involving a change from a.m. to p.m. or from p.m. to a.m. until activity 7.1e).
  - o Students use their clocks to find the answers. They can work in pairs, with one setting the start time and the other the end time. Then you draw a time line to show the same thing.

How long is it from 10:30 a.m. to 2:17 p.m.?

  - o It is not necessary to spend a lot of time on time lines here, since students are still using a clock face. They will also be used in Activity 7.1d, where students will be finding the duration of a time interval without clock faces.
- Give the students a start time and a time interval. Have them find the end time using their clocks.
- Students can work in pairs. Each sets a time on their clock. Both write down the time and include a.m. or p.m. They then use their clocks to find the duration of the time interval. If they both have a.m. or p.m., they go from the time with the smaller hour to the time with the larger hour. If one has a.m. and the other p.m., they can find the duration using either time as the start time.

Workbook Exercise 37

Activity 7.1c   **Convert between hours and minutes**

1. Convert hours to minutes.
   - Ask your students for the number of minutes in 1 hour. 2 hours? 3 hours? Continue up to 10 hours. Write the results on the board. Students should see that we multiply the hours by 60 to get the time in minutes.

1 hour	→ 60 minutes
2 hours	→ 120 minutes
3 hours	→ 180 minutes
4 hours	→ 240 minutes
5 hours	→ 300 minutes
6 hours	→ 360 minutes
7 hours	→ 420 minutes
8 hours	→ 480 minutes
9 hours	→ 540 minutes
10 hours	→ 600 minutes

   - Have your students practice counting by 60 up to 600. Point out that this is the same as counting by 6, but in tens, so there is an added 0.
   - Erase the table on the board. Ask your students to give you the number of minutes for random hours between 1 and 10. They can multiply the hours by 6 and then 10.

2. Convert hours and minutes to minutes.
   - Discuss **tasks 6-7, ^{US}p. 82 (^{3d}p. 69)** in the textbook. After doing task 7 have students add the times of the children in task 6 (4 h 40 min) and convert to minutes.
     - o To convert from hours and minutes to minutes, we multiply the hours by 60, and then add the minutes. 4 h 40 min = 240 min + 40 min = 280 min
   - Have students supply the answers for **task 8, ^{US}p. 82 (^{3d}p. 69)**.
   - Provide other problems for practice.

3. Convert minutes to hours.
   - Give students a number of minutes that is a multiple of 60, and ask them for the number of hours. For example, ask them how many hours are in 540 minutes.
   - Repeat with other multiples of 60 minutes.

4. Convert minutes to hours and minutes.
   - Discuss **task 9, ^{US}p. 82 (^{3d}p. 69)** in the textbook.
     o Students must find the multiple of 60 closest to but less than the number of hours. They can count up by 60, to that number, and then determine the number they counted by. For example, for 200 min, they count 60, 180, 240. 240 is too much. 180 is 2 hours. Then they subtract 180 from 200 to get the number of minutes.
   - Have students do **task 10, ^{US}p. 82 (^{3d}p. 69)**.
   - Provide other problems for practice.

Workbook Exercise 38

Activity 7.1d   **Convert between hours and minutes**
Game

Material for each group of students:
- 10 to 20 pairs of cards, one in each pair with the hours and minutes the other with the corresponding minutes.

Procedure:
- Cards are shuffled, placed face down in the middle, and the first one turned over.
- Students take turns turning over the next card and trying to match it with a face-up card. If there is no match, they leave it face-up on the table.
- Play continues until all cards have been matched.
- Students can also play a game like concentration. Cards are placed face-down in an array. Students take turns turning over two cards. If they match, they are removed from the array, if not, they are turned face down again.

Activity 7.1e   **Duration of time without a clock face**

1. Find the number of minutes up to the next hour.
   - Write down a time, such as 3:40, and ask students to tell you the number of minutes to the next hour, 4:00.
   - Repeat with other examples. Include some where the minutes are not a multiple of 5, such as 3:42. Students can count up by tens, and then ones to 60.

2. Find the duration of a time interval by using a time line and counting up.
   - Write down two times, such as 10:30 and 11:15, with a time interval of less than 60, but with the time going to the next hour.
     o Ask students for the number of minutes between those times. Show a time line for this.
     o We can first find the number of minutes up to the next hour, and then add on the minutes past that.

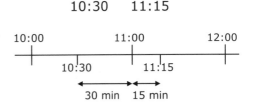

- Do some examples for durations of more than an hour. For example, write down 3:40 and 6:20.
  - o Use a time line to show how we can count by hours first (4:40, 5:40) then by minutes to the next hour (20 minutes from 5:40 to 6:00) and by minutes after the hour (20 minutes from 6:00 to 6:20). The total duration in this example is 2 hours 40 minutes.
  - o Students can keep track of the number of hours as they count up the hours using fingers.

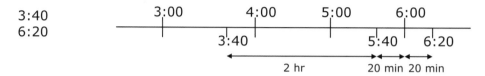

- Give them a problem that involves a change from a.m. to p.m. Here, they will find the duration by counting up. (In the next activity, they will find the interval using addition of compound units.) Counting up is easier to do than adding in compound units when there is no paper and pencil handy. For example, put a time-line on the board and mark 10:30 a. m. and 2:05 p.m.
  - o We can count first by hours to 12:30, and then switch over for the next hour to 1:30. 3 hours have passed so far. (Students can keep track of the number of hours that pass as they count up by using their fingers.)
  - o Then there are 30 minutes to the next hour plus 5 more minutes to 2:05. It is 3 hours and 35 minutes from 10:30 a.m. to 2:05 p.m.

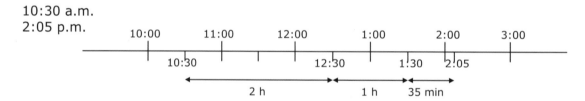

3. Find the end time when given the start time and the duration.
   - Give your students a start time and a duration where adding the minutes does not involve going to the next hour, and ask them to find the end time. For example, ask them to find 4 h 20 min after 6:30.
     - o Draw a time line. Mark one spot as 6:30, make 4 more marks to show 4 hours, and a mark close to the fourth mark to show 20 more min.
     - o Show how we can count up 4 hours from 6:30 to 10:30, and then add on 20 min to get to 10:40.

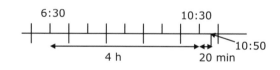

   - Give students a start time and a duration where the minutes will be more than 60, and ask them to find the end time. For example, ask them the find 4 h 40 min after 6:60.
     - o They can count up 4 hours from 6:30 to 10:30 as before. Lead them to see that adding another 40 minutes will bring them up to the next hour for the first 30 min, then past it by 10 min. 10:30, 11:00, 11:10. The end time is 11:10.

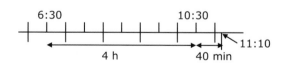

4. Find the start time given the end time and the duration.

- Give students time interval and an end time and ask them to find the start time. Keep the minutes of the duration less than the minutes in the end time. For example, ask them what the time was 2 h 10 min before 10:20.
  - o We can count back two hours to 8:20, then another 10 min to 8:10.
  - o You can illustrate with a time line.

5. Discuss **tasks 11-13, ^{US}p. 83 (^{3d}p. 70)** in the textbook.

Workbook Exercise 39

Activity 7.1f   **Add or subtract hours and minutes in compound units**

1. Discuss some problems where minutes are added and the sum of the minutes is greater than 60. 60 min will have to be renamed as 1 hour.

   - We need 30 more minutes to bring 3 h 30 min to the next hour (to make 60). Split 50 min into 30 min and 20 min.

     3 h 30 min + 50 min = 4 h 20 min
                       30 min 20 min

   - Or, we can add the minutes together, and then convert that sum into hours and minutes. This gives one more hour.

     3 h 30 min + 50 min

     30 min + 50 min = 80 min = 1 h 20 min

     3 h 30 min + 50 min = 3 h + 1 h 20 min
                                        = 4 h 20 min

2. Discuss some problems where both hours and minutes are added.
   - Add the hours first, then the minutes.
   - Add the minutes using the same strategies already learned.

     3 h 45 min + 2 h 30 min

                   + 2 h
     3 h 45 min ⟶ 5 h 45 min

                + 30 min
     5 h 45 min ⟶ 6 h 15 min
        15 min   30 min

     or:
       3 h 45 min
     + 2 h 30 min
       5 h 75 min → 6 h 15 min

3. Have students subtract minutes from one hour. Use minutes that are multiples of 5.

   1 h − 30 min = 30 min
   1 h − 45 min = 15 min
   1 h − 25 min = 35 min

4. Have students subtract minutes from hours and minutes where there are not enough minutes.
   We can subtract the minutes from one of the hours, and then add the difference to the remaining minutes.

   5 h 10 min − 45 min = 4 h 10 min + 15 min
                                 = 4 h 25 min
   4 h 10 min 1 h

   - Or, we can rename 5 h 10 min as 4 h 70 min and subtract 45 min from 70 min.

     5 h 10 min − 45 min
     = 4 h 70 − 45 min
     = 4 h 25 min

5. Discuss some problems where both hours and minutes are subtracted.
   - Subtract the hours first, then the minutes.
   - Subtract the minutes using the same strategies already learned.

5 h 20 min – 2 h 30 min

$$5 \text{ h } 20 \text{ min} \xrightarrow{- 2 \text{ h}} 3 \text{ h } 20 \text{ min}$$

$$3 \text{ h } 20 \text{ min} \xrightarrow{- 30 \text{ min}} 2 \text{ h } 50 \text{ min}$$

2 h 20 min   1 h

or:

5 h 20 min → 4 h 80 min
- 2 h 30 min
2 h 50 min

6. Discuss **tasks 14** and **16, ^{US}pp. 84-85 (^{3d}pp. 71-72)** in the textbook
   - Have students practice finding some other durations for intervals before 12:00 a.m. or p.m.

7. Discuss **task 15, ^{US}p. 84 (^{3d}p. 71)**.
   - We can count up to find how long the supermarket was open, remembering to change over from 12 (noon) to 1 rather than 12 to 13. Follow the time-line illustration, which shows the time above the line.
   - Or, we can add the amount of time to 12:00 noon to the amount of time after 12:00 noon. The duration is shown below the time line.

8. Discuss **task 17, ^{US}p. 85 (^{3d}p. 72)**.
   - Lead students to see that if we subtract the time from the start time to 12:00 midnight from the total time, the difference will give us the time after 12:00 midnight, which is the time the tour ended.

9. Students find the answers for **task 18, ^{US}p. 85 (^{3d}p. 72)**.

Workbook Exercise 40

Activity 7.1h   **Practice**

1. Use **Practice 7A, ^{US}p. 86 (^{3d}p. 73)** to review the concepts learned in this section. Students can work independently or in groups and then share their methods.

Part 2: Other Units of Time (^{US}pp. 87-89, ^{3d}pp. 74-76) **4 sessions**

Objectives

- Understand the second as a unit of measurement.
- Convert minutes and seconds to seconds and vice versa.
- Learn the months of the year.
- Learn the number of days in each month.
- Convert years and months to months and vice versa.

Materials

- Large analog clock with second hand.
- Stopwatches, one for each group of students.
- Large calendar with names of the month visible.
- Pairs of cards with years and months on one and the corresponding number of months on the other. A set of 10 to 20 pairs per group.
- Pairs of cards with weeks and days on one and the corresponding number of days on the other. A set of 10 to 20 pairs per group.
- A calendar page for each student.

Homework

- Workbook Exercise 41
- Workbook Exercise 42
- Workbook Exercise 43
- Workbook Exercise 44

Notes

In this section, students will learn how to carry out additional conversions involving minute to second, year to month, and week to day. They will also add or subtract time in minutes and seconds. The process is the same as for adding or subtracting time in hours and minutes.

Activity 7.2a   **Seconds**

1. Introduce seconds.
   - Use a large wall clock with a second hand. Have students watch the second hand and observe the relative movement of the minute and hour hands. They should note that the second hand goes around once for every minute.
   - Count the seconds as the second hand goes around. Lead students to see that 1 minute = 60 seconds.   1 minute = 60 seconds
   - If you can stop the second hand (take the battery out) have students tell time by 5-second intervals. For example, 4:32 and 10 seconds.
   - Show how this is written.
   - Some students may have watches (likely digital) that can act as stop watches, or that show the seconds. Have them observe the seconds on their watches.
   - Have students count by ones to 60 and see how many seconds have passed, and then count more slowly to get close to 60, using a long word in between, like "one one thousands, two one thousands,…" or "one white elephant, two white elephants…". Then they can count this way to approximate a minute.

2. Measure time in seconds.
   - Divide students into pairs or groups. Give each group a stopwatch, or let them use their watches as stopwatches. Get the students to time various activities, such as those in the textbook, US**p. 87** (3d**p. 17)**, or in the **workbook, exercise 41, problem 1**. Have them record their results.

3. Discuss **Workbook Exercise 41, #2-3** in class.

4. Discuss **task 2,** US**p. 88** (3d**p. 75)** in the textbook.
   - The process is the same as used in converting hours and minutes.
   - Provide other problems for practice.

Workbook Exercise 42

Activity 7.2b   **Months and years**

1. Discuss months. Post a list of months on the board.
   - Show students a calendar. Discuss years and months. Explain that the length of a year is the time it takes for the earth to go around the sun. As the earth goes around the sun, the seasons change. This takes 365 days. The total days of the year are divided into 12 months. Give them the date for this year and for last year. Ask them for the date next year.
   - Discuss when a new year starts.
   - Have student learn the names of the months.
     o Help them learn the months in order.
     o Give them a month's name and ask them to give you the name of the previous and the following month.
     o Have them find several months from a month, or several months before a month. Lead them to see that the months start over after December. So 3 months from November is February of the next year.
     o Review periodically in later lessons.

- Show them a newspaper with today's date. Remind them that a new paper comes every day, and the date is different each day.
- Write today's date as it is given in the newspaper. Write other dates in the same format. August 17,2004 (or 17 August, 2004)
- Have students find their birthdays on the calendar. Have them find various holidays. Write the dates of some of these.
- Optional: Discuss writing the date with only numbers (not writing out the month). Relate the number for the month to the month. 8/17/04 (or 17/8/04)
- Give students a number between 1 and 12 and have them name the month. They can use their fingers to count the months in order.
- Give students the name of a month and have them tell you the number for the month
- Go through the list of months discussing the number of days in each. Since every month does not have the same number of days, we can't convert the number of months to the number of days by just multiplying by a certain number.
- Optional: Discuss leap year.
  - Every fourth year, February has 29 days instead of 28. This is because it actually takes $365\frac{1}{4}$ days for the earth to go around the sun, not just 365 days. So every 4th year is called a Leap Year, and in that year February has one more day to catch up.

2. Convert from years and months to months.
   - Ask students for the number of months in 1 year. 2 years? 3 years? Lead them to see that they multiply the years by 12 to get the number of months.
   - Review the multiplication facts for 12.
     - Lead students to see that they can count by 12s by adding one ten and two ones.

   1 year = 12 months
   2 years = 2 x 12 = 24 months
   3 years = 3 x 12 = 36 months
   4 years = 4 x 12 = 48 months
   5 years = 5 x 12 = 60 months
   6 years = 6 x 12 = 72 months
   7 years = 7 x 12 = 84 months
   8 years = 8 x 12 = 96 months
   9 years = 9 x 12 = 108 months
   10 years = 10 x 12 = 120 months

   - Ask students for the number of months in 4 years 6 months.
     - We multiply the years by 12 months, and then add the months.
   - Give them some additional problems for practice.

   4 years 6 months = 48 months + 6 months
   = 54 months

3. Convert from months to years and months.
   - Give your students a multiple of 12 months up to 120 months and ask them for the number of years. Students have not yet learned to divide by a 2-digit number, but they should be able to recognize multiples of 12. You can limit the discussion to 4 or 5 years (up to 60 months).
   - Ask students for the number of years in 24 months. Then ask them for the number of years and months in 25 months. 26 months? 30 months? 37 months?

   25 months = 2 years 1 month

   24 months   1 month

4. Have students do **task 3, ^{US}p. 88 (^{3d}p. 75)** in the textbook.

Workbook Exercise 43

Activity 7.2e   **Weeks**

1. Discuss weeks.
   - Write the names for the days in the week on the board. Give each student a calendar page.
   - Have them count the number of days in a week.
   - Have the class read the names for the days of the week.
   - Give them a day of the week, such as Monday, and ask them for the day before and the day after, or several days before and several days after. Lead them to see that the day before Sunday is Saturday of the previous week, and the day after Saturday is Sunday of the next week.
   - Have them find a specific date on the calendar, and then the date 7 days later. Tell them that the second date is a week (7 days) after the first date. The week on the calendar starts with Sunday, but a week after Tuesday is the next Tuesday.
   - Show them how to read and write the date from the calendar, for example: Tuesday, August 17, 2004 (or Tuesday, 17 August, 2004).
   - Ask them what date would be before the first of the month and after the last. Show them the next month and how the rest of the week is on the next calendar page.

2. Convert from weeks and days to days.
   - Ask students for the number of days in 1 week. 2 weeks? 3 weeks? Lead them to see that they multiply the weeks by 7 to get the number of days.
   - Ask students for the total number of days in 4 weeks 6 days
     - We multiply the number of weeks by 7, and then add the number of days.

       $$4 \text{ weeks } 6 \text{ days} = 28 \text{ days} + 6 \text{ days} = 34 \text{ days}$$
   - Give them some additional problems for practice.

3. Convert from days to weeks and days.
   - Give your students a multiple of 7 up to 70 and ask them for the number of days. Lead them to see that they must divide by 7.
   - Ask students for the number of weeks in 21 days. Then ask them for the number of weeks and days in 22 days. 23 days? 24 days?

       $$24 \text{ days} = 3 \text{ weeks } 3 \text{ days}$$
       $$21 \text{ days} \quad 3 \text{ days}$$
     - We can divide the number of days by 7. The quotient is the number of weeks, and the remainder the number of days left.
   - Do some other examples.

4. Have students do **task 4, ^{US}p. 88 (^{3d}p. 75)** in the textbook.

Workbook Exercise 44

Activity 7.2f
Game

Version 1: Convert between years and months. Use 10-20 pairs of cards for each group, one card in each pair with the years and months and the other with the corresponding number of months.

Version 2: Convert between weeks and days. Use 10-20 pairs of cards for each group, one card in each pair with the weeks and days and the other with the corresponding number of days.

Material for each group:
- 10 to 20 pairs of cards as described above.

Procedure:
- Cards are shuffled, placed face down in the middle, and the first one turned over.
- Students take turns turning over the next card and trying to match it with a face-up card. If there is no match, they leave it face-up on the table.
- Play continues until all cards have been matched.
- Students can also play a game like concentration. Cards are placed face-down in an array. Students take turns turning over two cards. If they match, they are removed from the array, if not, they are turned face down again.
- You can mix in some of the cards from earlier games so that students are practicing with other conversion factors.

Activity 7.2h   **Practice**

1. Use **Practice 7B, ^{US}p. 89 (^{3d}p. 76)** in the textbook to review the concepts learned in this section. Students can work independently or in groups and then share their solutions.

Review

Objectives
- Review all topics.

Suggested number of sessions: 2

	Objectives	Textbook	Workbook	Activities
Review				**2 sessions**
66	▪ Review topics from Primary Mathematics.	^{US}pp. 90-91 ^{3dp}pp. 77-78	Review 7	R.4a
67				

Homework
- Workbook Review 7

Activity R.4a   **Review**

1. Have students work individually or in groups on the problems in **Review E**, ^{US}**pp. 90-91** (^{3d}**pp. 77-78)** and then have some share their solutions.

2. Review mental math or have students do some games from previous units.

Unit 8 – Geometry

Objectives

- Identify angles in the environment.
- Relate size of angles to the degree of turning.
- Relate the number of angles to the number of sides in a polygon.
- Identify right angles.
- Recognize that squares and rectangles have four right angles.
- Classify angles as less than, equal to, or greater than a right angle.

Suggested number of sessions: 3

	Objectives	Textbook	Workbook	Activities
Part 1 : Hours and Minutes				**2 sessions**
68	▪ Identify angles in the environment. ▪ Relate size of angles to the degree of turning.	US pp. 92-93 3d pp. 79-80		8.1a
69	▪ Relate the number of angles to the number of sides in a polygon	US p. 93 3d p. 80	Ex. 45	8.1b
Part 2 : Right Angles				**1 session**
70	▪ Identify right angles. ▪ Classify angles as less than, equal to, or greater than a right angle.	US pp. 94-95 3d pp. 81-82	Ex. 46	8.2a

Part 1: Angles (^{US}pp. 92-93, ^{3d}pp. 79-80)   **2 lessons**

Objectives

- Identify angles in the environment.
- Relate size of angles to the degree of turning.
- Relate the number of angles to the number of sides in a polygon.

Materials

- Two cards for each student. The cards should preferably be fairly stiff, such as thin cardboard. Fasten the cards to each other along the width to form a hinge.
- Two folding meter stick or two sets geostrips attached at one end, or two sets of two strips of cardboard attached at one end with a brad. See activity 8.1a
- Large cardboard polygonal shapes.

Homework

- Workbook Exercise 45

Notes

In this section, students will learn the concept of an angle.

An angle is formed when two straight lines meet at a point.

The size of an angle is determined by how much either line is turned about the point where they meet. It does not depend on the length of the two sides or arms.

A polygon is a closed figure formed by straight line segments. *Primary Mathematics 3B* will concentrate primarily on three special polygons: The rectangle, the square, and the triangle.

An angle is formed where any two sides of a polygon meet. The number of angles is equal to the number of sides. Right angles and comparing angles to right angles will be covered, but measurement of angles in degrees will be learned later, in *Primary Mathematics 4*.

Activity 8.1a   **Angles**

1. Discuss angles.
   - Use a folding meter stick or geostrips. Open it a little ways and show students the angle formed. Trace the angle on the board.
     - o Tell students that an angle is formed when two straight lines meet at a point.
   - Give each student two cards taped along one edge.
   - Have students use these to do the activity in the textbook, ^{US}**p. 92** (^{3d}**p. 79**).
   - Have students trace some of the angles formed if their cards are stiff enough.
   - Refer to **task 1, ^{US}p. 93 (^{3d}p. 80)**.
     - o Have students look around the classroom to find angles. You can call on students to go to the object containing the angle and place their cards against them or your folding ruler or geostrips to show the angle.

2. Relate the size of angles to the degree of turning.
   - Use a folding meter stick or geostrips.
     - o Start with it closed up, and then open to draw larger and larger angles.
     - o Lead students to see that the larger the angle, the more one side has to be turned away from the other side.

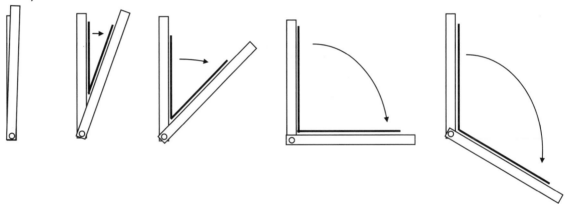

   - Have students locate angles in the environment again. Let two students use folding meter sticks or geostrips to measure the size of two angles and compare.
   - Use the folding meter stick to draw two angles the same size on the board.
     - o Ask students if the angles are the same size.
     - o Extend the arms of one of them.
     - o Ask them if the angles are still the same size.
     - o Lead students to see that the size of the angle does not depend on the length of the arms or sides.

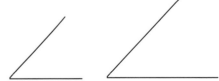

Activity 8.1b   **Angles in a polygon**

1. Discuss angles in a polygon.
   - Have students do **tasks 2-3, ^{US}p. 93 (^{3d}p. 80)** in the textbook.
   - Show students various shapes. Students can draw their own shapes with rulers. Shapes must be closed (with an inside and an outside and no way to get outside without crossing over a line) and have straight lines only. There is an angle wherever two sides meet. Angles are where two sides meet.
     o Have students count the number of angles and straight lines.
     o Get them to give you a general rule about the number of angles and the number of sides.   The number of angles equals the number of sides.
   - Have students use their hinged cards to compare the sizes of the angles in their figures. They can number the angles in order of size, with 1 for the smallest angle, two for the next larger, and so on. Point out that a figure can have different sizes of angles.

4 lines
4 angles

3 lines
3 angles

6 lines
6 angles

5 lines
5 angles

Workbook Exercise 45

Part 2: Right Angles (^{US}pp. 94-95, ^{3d}pp. 81-82) **1 session**

Objectives

- Identify right angles.
- Classify angles as less than, equal to, or greater than a right angle.

Materials

- Index cards for students.
- Large cardboard squares and rectangles and other shapes to show students.

Homework

- Workbook Exercise 46

Notes

In this section, students will learn to identify a right angle as a square corner.

Rectangles and squares have four right angles.

Angles can be classified as being less than, equal to, or greater than a right angle. Students will compare angles to a right angle using a square corner as a right angle.

Measurement of angles in degrees will be learned in *Primary Mathematics 4*.

Activity 8.2a   **Right angles**

1. Discuss right angles.
   - Students can do the activity on ^{US}p. 94 (^{3d}p. 81) in the textbook. Make sure they line up the edges with the second fold, or the angle won't be a right angle. You can give them an index card and tell them that the corner is a right angle. They can use that to check if their constructed angle is a right angle. They can use either their angle or the angle in and index card to check the other angles in this activity.
   - Have them use their square corner to find right angles around them in the environment. For example, the corners of a door, doorway, or window come together at right angles.
   - Have students use their square corners to determine whether an angle in their environment is less than, equal to, or greater than a right angle.
   - Use the demonstration clock. Have students determine whether the angle formed by the hour and minute hands is a right angle at various times.

2. Discuss right angles in rectilinear figures.
   - Have students do **task 1, ^{US}p. 95 (^{3d}p. 82)**.
   - Show students some other squares and rectangles including some that are rotated with respect to the board. Tell them that a square is a special rectangle whose sides are all the same length.
     - o Ask them for the number of right angles in these squares and rectangles. Lead them to see that they all have four right angles.
   - Have students do **task 2, ^{US}p. 95 (^{3d}p. 82)**.
     - o Draw or show some other triangles and have students tell you if one of the angles is greater than a right angle.
   - Have students do **task 3, ^{US}p. 95 (^{3d}p. 82)**.
     - o You can have them classify each angle as less than, equal to, or greater than a right angle.

3. Ask student how many right angles a four sided figure could have. Draw pictures to illustrate all the possible choices. (It can have 0, 1, 2, or 4 right angles. 3 right angles is not possible.)

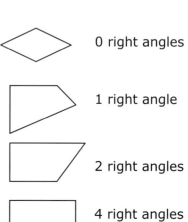

0 right angles

1 right angle

2 right angles

4 right angles

Workbook Exercise 46

Unit 9 – Area and Perimeter

Objectives

- Measure and compare areas in square units.
- Measure and compare areas in square centimeters.
- ^{US}Measure and compare areas in square inches.
- Understand the relative sizes of square centimeters and square meters
- ^{US}Understand the relative sizes of square inches, square feet, square yards, square miles, and acres.
- Find the perimeter of a rectilinear figure given its sides.
- Find the area of a rectangle given its length and width.
- Find the perimeter of a rectangle given its length and width.

Suggested number of sessions: 7

	Objectives	Textbook	Workbook	Activities
Part 1 : Area				**3 sessions**
71	• Find the area of a figure in square units. • Compare the area of figures in square units.	^{US}pp. 96-97 ^{3d}pp. 83-84	Ex. 47	9.1a
72	• Measure and compare area in square centimeters. • ^{US}Measure and compare area in square inches.	^{US}pp. 98-99 ^{3d}pp. 85-86	Ex. 48	9.1b 9.1c
73	• Measure area in square meters. • ^{US}Measure area in square feet and square yards. • Visualize and compare relative sizes in square centimeters, meters, inches, feet, and yards.	^{US}p. 100 ^{3d}p. 87	Ex. 49	9.1d
Part 2 : Perimeter				**2 sessions**
74	• Measure the perimeter of a figure. • Compare the area of figures to their perimeter	^{US}pp. 101-103 ^{3d}pp. 88-90	Ex. 50, #1-2	9.2a
75	• Find the perimeter of a rectilinear figure given the length of each side.	^{US}p. 104 ^{3d}p. 91	Ex. 50, #3	9.2b
Part 3 : Area of a Rectangle				**2 sessions**
76	• Find the area of a rectangle given the length of each side.	^{US}pp. 105-106 ^{3d}pp. 92-93	Ex. 51	9.3a
77	• Solve problems involving area and perimeter.	^{US}p. 107 ^{3d}p. 94	Ex. 52	9.3b

Part 1: Area ([US]pp. 96-100, [3d]pp. 83-87)	**3 sessions**

Objectives

- Measure and compare areas in square units.
- Measure and compare areas in square centimeters.
- [US]Measure and compare areas in square inches.
- Understand the relative sizes of square centimeters and square meters
- [US]Understand the relative sizes of square inches, square feet, square yards, square miles, and acres.

Materials

- Paper, plastic, or wooden squares and half squares (triangles) such as those from pattern blocks.
- Square centimeter paper.
- Square centimeter paper copied onto transparencies, one for each student or group of students.
- [US]Square inch paper.
- Rulers for each student.
- Four meter sticks.

Homework

- Workbook Exercise 47
- Workbook Exercise 48
- Workbook Exercise 49

Notes

Students were introduced to the concept of area in *Primary Mathematics 2B*. They measured and compared area in non-standard square units. Here they will measure area in standard units.

The area of a figure is the amount of flat space it covers. If the area of the figure is 4 cm^2, (square centimeters) then it covers the same amount of space as four squares each of whose sides measures 1 cm.

Square Inches

Square Centimeters

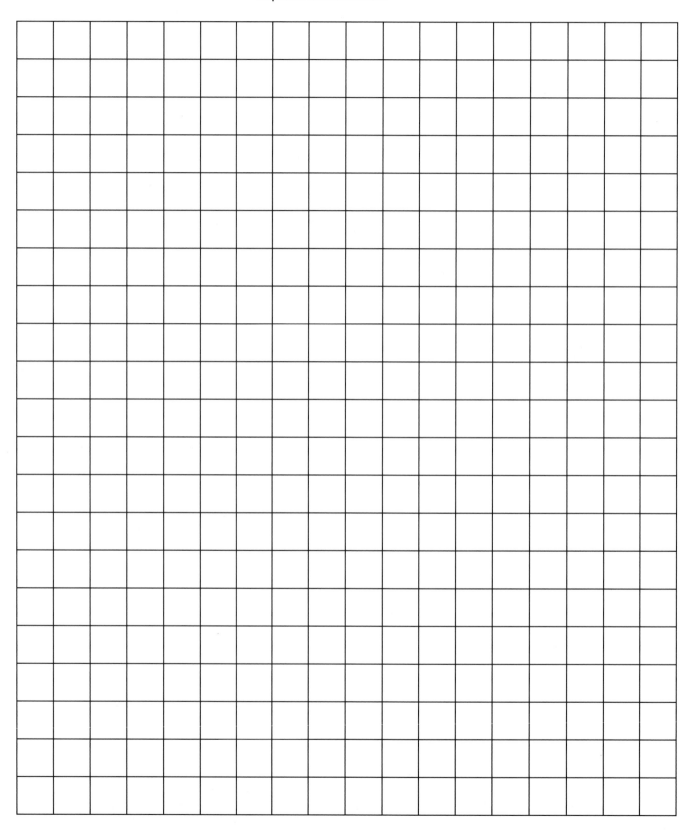

Activity 9.1a   **Area in non-standard units**

1. Discuss area.
   - Ask students to tell you what they think area is. Discuss area of a rug, room, driveway, parking lot, etc. Get them to see that area is the amount of flat space covered.
   - Ask them how we measure area. Some may remember square units from earlier math instruction.
   - Show students a paper square. Tell them that this covers one square unit.
   - Give each student the same number of squares, such as six. Have each student make a figure from them. They do not have to line up the edges, but all the squares must touch. Lead them to see that they all have the same area.
   - Discuss ^{US}p. 96 (^{3d}p. 83) in the textbook.
   - Give students two paper squares taped together or just draw it on the board. Draw a line as shown, and shade in one part. Ask students for the area of the shaded part. They can cut the parts apart and rearrange to show that the area is 1 square unit.
   - Have students do **task 1, ^{US}p. 97 (^{3d}p. 84)**.
   - Give students square centimeter paper. Have them draw figures using straight lines from corner to corner only, and then determine the areas.

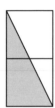

2. Discuss area of irregular figures.
   - Give students some centimeter graph paper. Have them trace some irregular object, such as the palm of their hand with fingers together, or the sole of their feet. Students can pair up to trace each other's feet. Ask them to find the area.
     - o They will only be able to find an approximate area. They can match edge pieces that make about a square unit with each other to count as one square unit.
   - Ask some students to give you their result. Tell them that when we say that the area of something is _____ square units, we mean that it covers that many square units, or that its size is the same as _____ square units.
   - Save for the next two activities.
   - Give each student or group of students square graph paper copied onto a transparency and have them lay it over drawings to estimate the area of the drawing.

Workbook Exercise 47

Activity 9.1b   **Area in standard units**

1. Discuss square centimeters as a standard unit of area.
   - Refer to **task 2, ^{US}p. 98 (^{3d}p. 85)** in the textbook.
     - o Have students use their rulers to measure the length of each side of the 1-cm square to confirm that they are 1 cm long.
     - o Tell students that the square centimeter is a standard unit for measuring area. Have students read it as *square centimeter*, not *c m 2*.
     - o Discuss the rest of task 2.
   - Draw 9 squares on the board in some other arrangement than 3 by 3.
     - o Ask students if the area is the same as that of the 3-cm square in the text. It is.
     - o Point out that saying that the area of a figure is 9 square centimeters doesn't mean the figure is a square; it just means that the total space it covers up is the same amount of space that would be covered up with 9 squares of 1 centimeter sides. The space could be rearranged into a square of length 3 cm.

- Give students centimeter graph paper. Have them use the paper to answer **task 3, [US]p. 98 ([3d]p. 85)**.

2. Have students measure and compare areas in square centimeters.
   - Have students do **task 4, [US]p. 99, [3d]p. 86**.
   - Give students some square centimeter paper. Give them an area, such as 10 cm^2, and have them draw a figure with that area. They can compare their figures.
   - Refer to the figure they traced, perhaps of the palms of their hands or soles of their feet, in the previous activity. Since they used square centimeter paper, they can give the area in square centimeters.

[US]3. Discuss square inches.
   - Give students square inch paper. They can measure the side of one of the squares with their rulers. Tell them that in the U.S., area is also measured in square inches as well as square centimeters.

     1 square inch = 1 in.^{2}

   - Square inches are written **in.^{2}**
   - Have them compare a square inch to a square centimeter.
   - They can trace their hands or feet on square inch paper, and compare the area to the area they found using square centimeter paper.
   - Give them a measurement in square inches and have them draw a figure on the square inch paper with that area.
   - Have them trace a regular object, such as a book, on square inch paper by lining up two sides with the edges of the squares and tracing around the book. Get them to find the area of the book.

Workbook Exercise 48

Activity 9.1c   **Explore area**
Group activity

Material for each group:
- Provide each group with centimeter graph paper.

Procedure:
- Get students to draw as many figures they can with an area of 5 square centimeters. Let them come up with as many unique shapes as they can. There are only 12 unique shapes. It may look like there are more, but show that those are actually the same as one of those 12, flipped or rotated. (See the next page for the 12 shapes.)
- Students can cut out each unique shape and combine the shapes into other shapes.

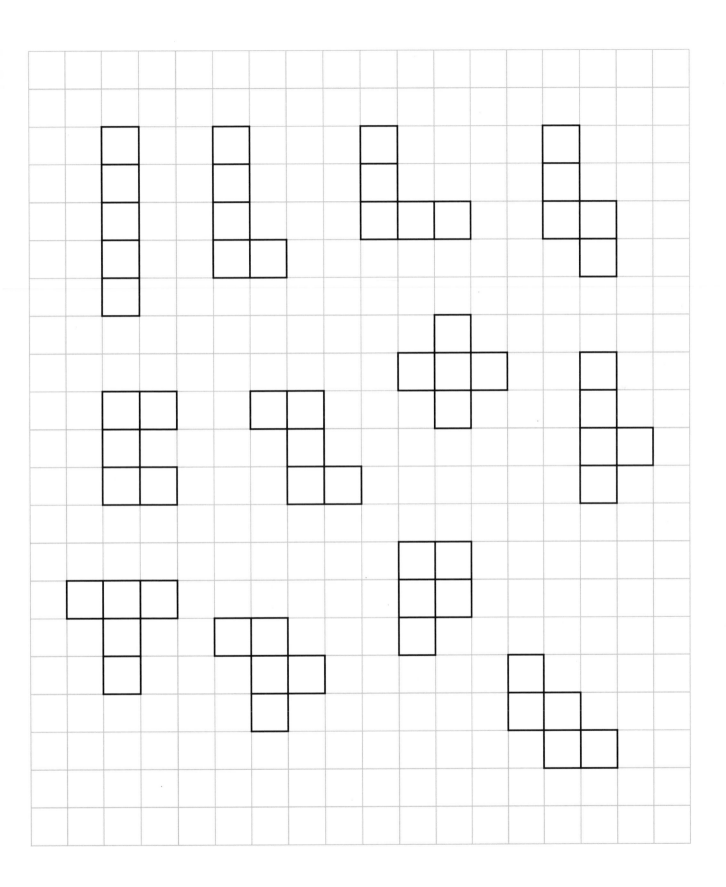

Activity 9.1d　　　　　　　　　　　　　　**Area in other standard units**

1. Discuss square meters.
   - Lay out 4 meter sticks in a square on the floor, or draw a square of side 1 meter.
     - Ask students for the length of each side in meters. Each side is 1 m.
     - Tell students that this is a square meter.
   - Have them compare the size of a square meter with a square centimeter.
   - You can have them find out how many people can stand in the square meter, or how many notebooks would fill a square meter.
   - Have groups of students tape sheets of paper together to form a square meter.
     - They can use this square to find the approximate area of the classroom floor, or the hall, or a tennis court.
   - Discuss ^{US}**p. 100,** ^{3d}**p. 87** in the textbook.
     - It is important to pay attention to the unit (meter or centimeter or other unit) which is given for the length of the side.
     - Point out that the square on this page is a scaled down picture of a square meter. Explain that this is similar to a map, which shows a road or even a whole city on one piece of paper. In the same way, pictures in our textbook need not be the actual size of the figures.
   - Optional: You may want to discuss other units for measuring area in the metric system.
     - A square kilometer is a square with 1000 meters on each side.
     - A hectare is a square with 100 meters on each side.

^{US}2. Discuss square feet and yards.
   - Use a ruler to draw a square foot on the board. Label each side as 1 foot.　　　　　　　　　　1 square foot = 1 ft^2
     - Tell students this is a square foot.
     - Tell students that the area of a room is often given in square feet.
     - Draw a square inch on the board and have them compare the size of a square inch to a square foot.
   - Lay out 4 yard sticks in a square on the floor, or draw a square of side 1 yard.
     - Ask students for the length of each side in yards.　　1 square yard = 1 yd^2 Each side is 1 yd.
     - Tell students that this is a square yard and is written as 1 yd^2.
   - They can compare the size of a square yard with a square foot.
   - You can use the paper square meter they made to compare a square yard to a square meter.
   - You can discuss other units for measuring area.
     - An acre is an area that can be covered with 4840 square yards.
     - A square mile is an area that can be covered with 640 acres.

Workbook Exercise 49

Part 2: Perimeter (^{US}pp. 101-105, ^{3d}pp. 88-92) 2 sessions

Objectives

- Find the perimeter of a figure.
- Find the perimeter of a polygon when given the length of its sides.
- Relate perimeter to area.

Materials

- Square centimeter paper.
- ^{US}Square inch paper.
- String.
- Rulers for each student.
- Copies of rectilinear shapes for each student. The shapes should have sides that measure to a whole or half centimeter (or inch).

Homework

- Workbook Exercise 50

Notes

Perimeter is introduced in this section.

The perimeter of a figure is the distance around the outside of the figure.

Students will use a string to measure the perimeter of figures with curved sides.

To find the perimeter of a rectilinear figure drawn with squares, the students will count up the units of length along the outside. They will need to be careful to count each unit length only once, and not to count a square corner as only one unit. They can mark off the units as they count them with a pencil mark.

Different shapes may have the same area but different perimeters, or the same perimeter but different areas, or two shapes could have the same perimeter and area but be different shapes.

If the length of the sides is measured or given, we find the perimeter by adding up the lengths of the sides.

The unit of measurement can be any of the standard units. Make sure the students understand that the figures are scaled down.

Activity 9.2a   **Perimeter**

1. Discuss perimeter.
   - Write on the board "PERIMETER = distance around". Explain that "perimeter" comes from Greek: PERI means "distance around" and METREO means "to measure". When we measure the distance around a figure, we are finding its perimeter.
   - Draw or display a 3 x 5 rectangle, showing the unit squares. Tell them that the squares are square centimeters.

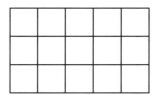

Area = 15 cm^2
Perimeter = 16 cm

   - o Ask students for the area. Write their answer on the board. (Area = 15 cm^2)
   - o Ask students for its perimeter. Remind students that the area was the space inside the figure, and now we are going to find the distance around it.
   - o Emphasize that you are not counting the number of squares, the way you do for area. They can imagine a small bug that must crawl around the edge of the figure; the perimeter is the distance the bug would have to travel.
   - o Discuss their answer. Count the unit length with them as you go around the figure, to show the correct answer. Write on the board "Perimeter = 16 cm".
   - o Emphasize that perimeter is measured in units of length (centimeters) whereas area is measured in square units (square centimeters).
   - Discuss the activity on ^{US}**p. 101** (^{3d}**p. 88**) in the textbook.
   - o Have students find the perimeter of each figure using rulers.
   - o Have them find the area of each figure.
   - o Note that figures can have the same perimeter, but different areas.

2. Have students do **tasks 1-5, ^{US}p. 102-103 (^{3d}pp. 89-90)**, one task at a time.
   - Discuss each task and its solution with them. Spend extra time with task 5.
   - o Figures can have the same area but different perimeters.
   - o Figures can have the same perimeter but different areas.
   - o Figures with the same area and perimeter can have different shapes.

3. Explore perimeter and area.
   - Give students some centimeter graph paper.
   - Have students look again at **task 3, ^{US}p. 102 (^{3d}p. 89)**. Get them to draw other, different figures with the same areas (6 cm^2).

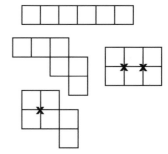

   - o Have them see if they can predict which figures will have a smaller perimeter, and then verify by counting unit lengths.
   - o See if they can tell that the fewer outside edges the figure has, the smaller the perimeter.
   - o They can cut out their figures and arrange them in order of their perimeters.
   - Have students look again at **task 3, ^{US}p. 102 (^{3d}p. 89)**. Have them draw on their graph paper figures R and S, or P and T, which have the same perimeter but different areas.
   - o Have them see if they can come up with a third figure with the same perimeter but a different area.
   - o They can cut out their figures and arrange them in order of their areas.

Workbook Exercise 50, #1-2

Activity 9.2b   **Perimeter of a polygon**

1. Find the perimeter of a square, given the length of one side.
   - Draw a 4 by 4 square and label the length of its sides.
   - Ask students for the perimeter, which they find by counting the unit lengths.
   - Erase the inside lines.
   - Ask them how they could find the perimeter without the unit squares.
   - Lead them to see that they can add the sides.
   - Since a square has equal sides, they can also multiply one side by 4 to get the perimeter.
   - Draw another square and label one side with a length in a standard measurement, such as 10 cm, or 3 feet, and have students tell you the perimeter.

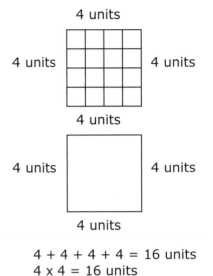

4 + 4 + 4 + 4 = 16 units
4 x 4 = 16 units

2. Find the perimeter of a rectangle, given the length of its sides.
   - Follow a procedure similar to that used with a square.
   - Lead students to see that they can find the perimeter by adding the sides.
   - See if they can come up with a different way of finding the perimeter. They can add the length and the width, and multiply the sum by 2.
   - Draw another rectangle, label the width and length in a standard measurement, and have students tell you the perimeter.

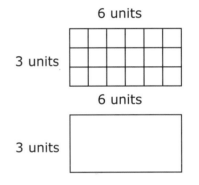

6 + 3 + 6 + 3 = 18 units
3 + 6 = 9
2 x 9 = 18 units

3. Students do **tasks 6-7, ^{US}p. 104 (^{3d}p. 91)** in the textbook.
   - Tell students to always write the unit of measurement with their answers.

4. Find perimeters.
   - Students can work in pairs or groups to measure the sides of various rectilinear figures, such as their texts, or desktops, to the nearest unit of measurement and then find the perimeter.
     o Groups can record their answers and compare with other groups.

Workbook Exercise 50, #3

Part 3: Area of a Rectangle (^{US}pp. 105-107, ^{3d}pp. 92-94)   **2 sessions**

Objectives

- Find the area of a rectangle given its length and width.
- Solve word problems involving area and perimeter.

Materials

- Square centimeter paper.
- Paper squares or connect-a-cubes or unit cubes.

Homework

- Workbook Exercise 51
- Workbook Exercise 52

Notes

In this section, students will learn to find the area of a rectangle by multiplying its length by its width.

Area of a rectangle = length x width

A square is a rectangle whose length is the same as its width.

Area of a square = side x side

Activity 9.3a   **Area of a rectangle**

1. Find the area of a rectangle.
   - Give each student centimeter graph paper and 24 paper squares (or connect-a-cubes or unit cubes). You can have the students work in pairs or groups.
     - o Have them make as many different rectangles as they can with the 24 squares. Have them draw each new rectangle on the centimeter graph paper.
     - o Get students to write down the length and width of each of their rectangles.
     - o Get students to find the area of each of their rectangles.
     - o Ask students whether they notice anything about the length and width of each rectangle. Lead them to see that length x width is 24 for each rectangle.
     - o Lead them to see that the length (or width) is the number of columns, and the width (or length) is the number of rows of squares. The total number of squares is the number of rows x the number of columns, or the length x the width. The total number of squares is the area. So we can find the area of a rectangle by multiplying the length by the width.

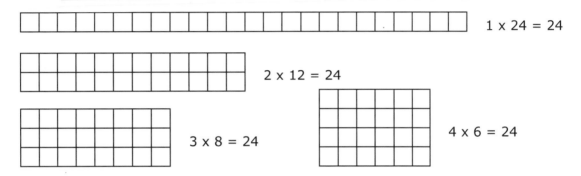

1 x 24 = 24

2 x 12 = 24

3 x 8 = 24

4 x 6 = 24

   - Discuss ^{US}**p. 105** (^{3d}**p. 92**) in the textbook.
   - Students do **tasks 1-2**, ^{US}**p. 106** (^{3d}**p. 93**).
     - o Get students to find the perimeters of the rectangles in 2(c) and 2(d) as well.

2. Find the area of a square.
   - Draw a square on the board and label one side with a length.
     - o Ask students to find the area of the square.
     - o Lead them to see that since a square is a special rectangle with all the sides equal, we only need to know the length of one side to find the area. The other side will be the same.
     - o Have students find the perimeter as well.
     - o Remind them to always write the unit of measurement. Here, area is in cm^2 and perimeter is in cm.
   - Draw a square on the board and label the size as 1 m.
     - o Ask students for the area.
     - o Draw a centimeter square in one corner to scale. Ask students for the area in square centimeters.
     - o Lead them to see that since the side of the square meter is 100 cm, the area is 100 cm x 100 cm = 10,000 cm.

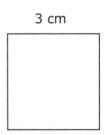

3 cm

Area = 3 cm x 3 cm = 9 cm^2
Perimeter = 4 x 3 cm = 12 cm

1 m^2 = 100 cm x 100 cm
      = 10,000 cm^2

- [US]Similarly, lead students to see that a square yard is 9 square feet and a square foot is 144 square inches.

$$1 \text{ yd}^2 = 3 \text{ ft} \times 3 \text{ ft}$$
$$= 9 \text{ ft}^2$$
$$1 \text{ ft}^2 = 12 \text{ in.} \times 12 \text{ in.}$$
$$= 144 \text{ in.}^2$$
$$1 \text{ yd}^2 = 9 \times 144 \text{ in.}^2$$
$$= 1296 \text{ in.}^2$$

Workbook Exercise 51

Activity 9.3b
Solve problems involving area and perimeter.

1. Students do **Practice 9A, [US]p. 107 ([3d]p. 94)** in the textbook.
   - Have students solve the problems individually and then share their methods and answers.
   - Provide other problems for practice.
   - Get students to make up some problems involving area or perimeter of rectangles to ask the rest of the class.

Workbook Exercise 52

Review

Objectives
- Review all topics.

Suggested number of sessions: 3

	Objectives	Textbook	Workbook	Activities
Review				**3 sessions**
78	▪ Review topics from Primary Mathematics.	^{US}pp. 108-109 ^{3d}pp. 95-96	Review 8 Review 9	R.5a
79				
80				

Homework
- Workbook Review 8
- Workbook Review 9

Activity R.5a   **Review**

1. Have students work individually or in groups on the problems in **Review F, ^{US}pp. 108-109 (^{3d}pp. 95-96)** and then have some share their solutions.

2. Review mental math or have students do some games from previous units.

Textbook Answer Key

Unit 1 - Mental Calculation

1 Addition (pp. 6-7)

1. (a) 33; 37; 37
   (b) 84; 90; 90
   (c) 78; 83; 83
2. (a) 71　　(b) 114
3. (a) 73　　(b) 87　　(c) 135
   (d) 77　　(e) 40　　(f) 72
   (g) 59　　(h) 62　　(i) 81
4. 74
5. (a) 66　　(b) 92　　(c) 110

2 Subtraction (pp. 8-9)

1. (a) 55; 53; 53
   (b) 36; 30; 30
   (c) 43; 35; 35
2. (a) 49　　(b) 46
3. (a) 40　　(b) 25
   (c) 8　　(d) 52
   (e) 80　　(f) 38
4. (a) 16　　(b) 30
   (c) 26　　(d) 32
   (e) 40　　(f) 8
5. 72
6. (a) 2　　(b) 4
   (c) 5　　(d) 33
   (e) 11　　(f) 22
   (g) 24　　(h) 12
   (i) 51

3 Multiplication (p. 10)

1. (a) 300　　(b) 1200
2. (a) 56　　(b) 560　　(c) 5600
   (d) 450　　(e) 320　　(f) 540
   (g) 1800　　(h) 1500　　(i) 2800

4 Division (p. 11)

1. (a) 20　　(b) 300
2. (a) 3　　(b) 30　　(c) 300
   (d) 20　　(e) 60　　(f) 40
   (g) 40　　(h) 600　　(i) 200

Practice 1A (p. 12)

1. (a) 93　　(b) 100　　(c) 102
2. (a) 198　　(b) 197　　(c) 72
3. (a) 33　　(b) 34　　(c) 5

4. (a) 1　　(b) 8　　(c) 1
5. (a) 120　　(b) 400　　(c) 1800
6. (a) 100　　(b) 60　　(c) 200
7. (a) 600　　(b) 450　　(c) 2100
8. (a) 20　　(b) 80　　(c) 90
9. (a) 600　　(b) 240　　(c) 2500
10. (a) 55　　(b) 242
    (c) 510　　(d) 5494
11. 480
12. 40
13. 280

Practice 1B (p. 13)

1. (a) 150　　(b) 300　　(c) 180
2. (a) 20　　(b) 20　　(c) 200
3. (a) 540　　(b) 2800　　(c) 2400
4. (a) 30　　(b) 40　　(c) 80
5. $400
6. 50
7. 360
8. 1200
9. (a) 50　　(b) $100
10. (a) 160　　(b) 20

Unit 2 - Length

1 Meters and Centimeters (pp. 14-17)

1. (a) 25　　(b) 125
2. (a) 200　　(b) 3
4. 145
5. (a) 190 cm　(b) 155 cm　(c) 286 cm
   (d) 289 cm　(e) 308 cm　(f) 406 cm
6. 3 m 95 cm
7. (a) 1 m 80 cm　　(b) 1 m 95 cm
   (c) 2 m 62 cm　　(d) 2 m 99 cm
   (e) 3 m 4 cm　　(f) 4 m 9 cm
8. 1 m 89 cm, 1 m 96 cm, 2 m 8 cm

Practice 2A (p. 18)

1. (a) 400 cm　(b) 140 cm　(c) 225 cm
   (d) 395 cm　(e) 405 cm　(f) 909 cm
2. (a) 1 m 20 cm　　(b) 2 m 25 cm
   (c) 3 m 9 cm　　(d) 6 m 18 cm
   (e) 9 m 63 cm　　(f) 4 m 5 cm
3. (a) 35 cm　　(b) 45 cm
   (c) 25 cm　　(d) 1 m 5 cm
   (e) 8 cm　　(f) 3 m 34 cm

4. (a) 5 m 75 cm   (b) 3 m 69 cm
    (c) 3 m 91 cm   (d) 6 m 3 cm
    (e) 85 cm   (f) 5 m 14 cm
    (g) 1 m 5 cm   (h) 81 cm
5. 1 m 44 cm
6. 3 m 45 cm

2 Kilometers (pp. 19-22)

1. (a) 1 km 10 m   (b) 1 km 750 m
2. (a) 42 km; 23 km   (b) 41 km
3. 6100 m
4. 1 km 200 m
5. (a) 1600 m   (b) 2550 m
    (c) 2605 m   (d) 3085 m
    (e) 3020 m   (f) 4005 m
6. (a) 1 km 830 m   (b) 2 km 304 m
    (c) 2 km 780 m   (d) 3 km 96 m
    (e) 3 km 40 m   (f) 4 km 9 m
8. 120 m

Practice 2B (p. 23)

1. (a) 3000 m   (b) 1450 m
    (c) 2506 m   (d) 2060 m
    (e) 3078 m   (f) 4009 m
2. (a) 1 km 680 m   (b) 1 km 85 m
    (c) 2 km 204 m   (d) 3 km 90 m
    (e) 3 km 999 m   (f) 4 km 1 m
3. (a) 200 m   (b) 400 m
    (c) 955 m   (d) 960 m
    (e) 60 m   (f) 1 km 725 m
4. (a) 5 km 650 m   (b) 3 km 510 m
    (c) 4 km 100 m   (d) 6 km
    (e) 1 km 950 m   (f) 4 km 100 m
    (g) 2 km 675 m   (h) 1 km 50 m
5. 1 km 460 m

US3 Yards, Feet and Inches (USpp. 24-26)

1. (a) 2   (b) 5
2. (a) 24   (b) 6
3. 35 ft
4. 5
5. (a) 5   (b) 17
6. (a) 84
7. Answers will vary
8. (a) 6 ft 5 in. (b) 2 ft 9 in.

US4 Miles (USp. 27)

1. 21 mi
2. 2930 mi   1670 mi

USPractice 2C (USp. 28)

1. (a) 15 ft
    (b) 263 ft
    (c) 925 ft
2. (a) 108 in.
    (b) 82 in.
    (c) 117 in.
3. (a) 9 yd 0 ft
    (b) 36 yd 0 ft
    (c) 70 yd 2 ft
4. (a) 1 ft 0 in.
    (b) 1 ft 4 in.
    (c) 2 ft
5. (a) 1 ft   (b) 2 ft   (c) 1 ft
    (d) 5 in.   (e) 4 in.
6. (a) 5 yd 2 ft   (b) 9 yd 1 ft
    (c) 8 yd 0 ft   (d) 1 yd 2 ft
    (e) 8 yd 2 ft   (f) 0 yd 2 ft
7. (a) 12 ft 11 in.   (b) 9 ft 11 in.
    (c) 12 ft 3 in.   (d) 11 ft 5 in.
    (e) 9 ft 10 in.   (f) 1 ft 10 in.

Unit 3 - Weight

1 Kilograms and Grams (USpp. 29-32 3dpp. 24-27)

    800 g   1 kg 300 g
1. (a) 1 kg   (b) 1 kg 200 g
    (c) 900 g   (d) 1 kg 700 g
2. 2200 g
3. 1 kg 400 g
4. 150 g; 150 g
5. chicken, 150 g
6. (a) 4 kg 100 g   (b) 1 kg 100 g

Practice 3A (USp. 33 3dp. 28)

1. (a) 1456 g   (b) 2370 g   (c) 3808 g
    (d) 2080 g   (e) 1008 g   (f) 4007 g
2. (a) 2 kg 143 g   (b) 1 kg 354 g
    (c) 3 kg 800 g   (d) 2 kg 206 g
    (e) 3 kg 85 g   (f) 4 kg 9 g
3. (a) 605 g   (b) 915 g
    (c) 600 g   (d) 940 g
    (e) 460 g   (f) 2 kg 195 g
4. (a) 5 kg 500 g   (b) 5 kg 100 g
    (c) 5 kg   (d) 6 kg 120 g
    (e) 2 kg 810 g   (f) 3 kg 250 g
    (g) 2 kg 750 g   (h) 2 kg 95 g
5. 6 kg 250 g
6. (a) 7 kg 190 g   (b) 1 kg 210 g

2 More Word Problems
(^{US}pp. 34-37 ^{3d}pp. 29-32))

    850 g
1. 255 g
2. 860 g
3. 19 kg; 19 kg
4. 4750 g; 4 kg 750 g
5. 33 kg 800 g
6. (a) 5 kg   (b) 1 kg 400 g
7. (a) 2 kg 650 g   (b) 4 kg 700 g
8. 450 g
9. 400 g
10. 4 kg; 1 kg 50 g

Practice 3B (^{US}p. 38 ^{3d}p. 33)

1. (a) 5000 g (b) 1950 g (c) 1060 g
   (d) 2805 g (e) 2005 g (f) 3002 g
2. (a) 1 kg 905 g   (b) 1 kg 55 g
   (c) 2 kg 208 g   (d) 3 kg 390 g
   (e) 3 kg 599 g   (f) 5 kg 2 g
3. (a) 3 kg 240 g   (b) 5 kg 100 g
   (c) 2 kg 520 g   (d) 2 kg 570 g
4. (a) 5 kg 70 g   (b) 970 g
5. 53 kg 460 g
6. 84 kg
7. 51 kg

^{US}3 Pounds and Ounces (^{US}pp. 39-41)

    8 oz 1 lb 11 oz
1. (a) 2 lb   (b) 7 lb 4 oz
2. 77 oz
3. 1 lb 8 oz
4. potatoes
5. (a) 5 lb 7 oz   (b) 1 lb 11 oz

^{US}Practice 3C (^{US}p. 42)

1. (a) 80 oz (b) 127 oz (c) 153 oz
2. (a) 1 lb 0 oz
   (b) 1 lb 4 oz
   (c) 1 lb 10 oz
3. (a) 8 lb 3 oz   (b) 9 lb 6 oz
   (c) 3 lb 14 oz   (d) 1 lb 2 oz
4. 8 lb 7 oz
5. 14 oz
6. 24 lb
7. (a) 6 lb 1 oz   (b) 13 oz

Review A (^{US}p. 43 ^{3d}p. 34)

1. (a) 541   (b) 4100   (c) 3147
2. (a) 605   (b) 1724   (c) 7004

3. (a) 371   (b) 780   (c) 1628
4. (a) 29   (b) 13   (c) 54
5. 192
6. $90
7. 20
8. 168
9. 36
10. 144

Review B (^{US}p. 44 ^{3d}p. 35)

1. (a) 500 cm   (b) 408 cm
   (c) 2560 m   (d) 3005 m
   (e) 1030 g   (f) 2080 g
2. (a) 2 m 8 cm   (b) 3 m 20 cm
   (c) 1 km 850 m   (d) 2 km 4 m
   (e) 3 kg 95 g   (f) 4 kg 209 g
3. (a) 2 m 28 cm   (b) 5 m 40 cm
   (c) 65 cm   (d) 2 m 20 cm
4. (a) 6 km 210 m   (b) 10 km 200 m
   (c) 8 km 640 m   (d) 4 km 550 m
5. (a) 5 kg 45 g   (b) 8 kg 110 g
   (c) 1 kg 180 g   (d) 1 kg 795 g
6. (a) 330 g (b) 240 g (c) 120 g

Unit 4 - Capacity

1 Liters and Milliliters
(^{US}pp. 45-50 ^{3d}pp. 36-41)

    (a) 750 ml (b) 2 ℓ 300 ml
3. 2 liters
4. (a) 350 ml (b) 800 ml (c) 1 ℓ 200 ml
6. 1100 ml; 1 ℓ 100 ml
7. 1 ℓ 500 ml
8. (a) 1 ℓ 200 ml   (b) 2 ℓ 500 ml
   (c) 2 ℓ 50 ml   (d) 1 ℓ 5 ml
   (e) 3 ℓ 400 ml   (f) 3 ℓ 105 ml
9. (a) 2000 ml   (b) 2350 ml
10. (a) 1800 ml
   (b) 1080 ml
   (c) 1008 ml
   (d) 3025 ml
   (e) 2005 ml
   (f) 3500 ml
11. 1 ℓ 250 ml
12. 350 ml
13. A; 260 ml

Practice 4A (^{US}p. 51 ^{3d}p. 42)

1. (a) 3000 ml   (b) 1200 ml
   (c) 2055 ml   (d) 2650 ml
   (e) 3065 ml   (f) 4005 ml

2. (a) 5 ℓ   (b) 1 ℓ 600 ml
    (c) 2 ℓ 250 ml   (d) 3 ℓ 205 ml
    (e) 2 ℓ 74 ml
    (f) 1 ℓ 9 ml
3. (a) more than
    (b) equal to
    (c) less than
4. (a) 2 ℓ   (b) 4 ℓ
    (c) 4 ℓ 50 ml   (d) 9 ℓ 140 ml
    (e) 1 ℓ 20 ml   (f) 2 ℓ 150 ml
    (g) 2 ℓ 720 ml   (h) 3 ℓ 925 ml
5. (a) Container A
    (b) Container B
    (c) 8 ℓ 30 ml

Practice 4B (^{US}p. 52 ^{3d}p. 43)

1. (a) 7 ℓ 950 ml   (b) 2 ℓ 650 ml
2. 4 ℓ 400 ml
3. 18 ℓ
4. 30 ℓ
5. 8
6. 3 ℓ 350 ml
7. 15 ℓ 600 ml

^{US}2 Gallons, Quarts, Pints and Cups (^{US}pp. 53-55)

2. 4 cups
3. 5 qt = 1 gal 1 qt
4. 19 gal 2 qt
5. 7 qt 1 pt
6. 10 pt 1 c
7. 2 qt 1 pt
8. 6 pt 0 qt

^{US}Practice 4C (^{US}p. 56)

1. (a) 16 c   (b) 31 c
2. (a) 14 pt   (b) 23 pt
3. (a) 40 qt   (b) 93 qt
4. (a) >   (b) >   (c) =
5. (a) 11 qt 0 pt
    (b) 4 gal 3 qt
    (c) 72 pt 1 c
6. 5 gal 3 qt
7. 3 pt
8. 7 pt

Review C (^{US}p. 57 ^{3d}p. 44)

1. (a) 5932   (b) 6808   (c) 3600
2. (a) 999   (b) 2924   (c) 5336
3. (a) 308   (b) 657   (c) 615
4. (a) 450   (b) 136   (c) 64 R6

5. 63
6. $2628
7. 80
8. 973
9. (a) 25   (b) $250

Unit 5 - Graphs

1 Bar Graphs (^{US}pp. 58-63 ^{3d}pp. 45-50)

^{US}Matthew - 4; Pablo - 6; Sam - 2; Tyrone – 9
        4   6   2   9
        21   2   2   Tyrone   Sam
^{3d}Minghua - 4; Rohan - 6; Samy - 2; Yonghua - 9
        4   6   2   9
        21   2   2   Yonghua   Samy
^{US}1. (a) 75   (b) 80   (c) 5
    (d) Mathematics, Social Studies
    (e) Science (f) Science (g) English
^{3d}1. (a) 75   (b) 80   (c) 5
    (d) Mathematics, Malay
    (e) Science (f) Science (g) English
2. (a) 20   (b) 40   (c) July
    (d) June   (e) June   (f) $125
3. (a) 60   (b) 75   (c) 25
    (d) Hassan   (e) David   (f) Mary
4. (a) 320   (b) 190   (c) Wed.
    (d) Thu.   (e) Tue.   (f) 120

Unit 6 - Fractions

1 Fraction of a Whole (^{US}pp. 64-68 ^{3d}pp. 51-55)

1. (a) 2; 5; two
    (b) 3; 5; three
    (c) five; 5
2. (a) $\frac{5}{8}$

    (b) eight; 8

    (c) $\frac{5}{8}$

3. (a) $\frac{1}{5}$ (b) $\frac{1}{6}$

    (c) $\frac{1}{12}$ (d) $\frac{2}{3}$

    (e) $\frac{2}{5}$ (f) $\frac{5}{6}$

    (g) $\frac{7}{8}$ (h) $\frac{7}{10}$

4. (a) 2 is the numerator
        5 is the denominator
    (b) 4 is the numerator
        10 is the denominator

(c) 6 is the numerator
    7 is the denominator
(d) 6 is the numerator
    9 is the denominator

5. $\frac{1}{3}$

6. $\frac{3}{4}$

7. $\frac{5}{8}$

8. $\frac{3}{10}$; $\frac{3}{5}$

9. $\frac{3}{9}$; $\frac{7}{9}$

10. (a) $\frac{1}{7}$, $\frac{1}{5}$, $\frac{1}{3}$ (b) $\frac{2}{9}$, $\frac{2}{7}$, $\frac{2}{3}$

    (c) $\frac{4}{8}$, $\frac{5}{8}$, $\frac{7}{8}$ (d) $\frac{4}{12}$, $\frac{5}{12}$, $\frac{9}{12}$

Practice 6A (^{US}p. 69, ^{3d}p. 56)

1. (a) $\frac{3}{4}$ (b) $\frac{7}{10}$ (c) $\frac{5}{12}$

2. (a) 2   (b) 6   (c) 9

3. (a) 8   (b) 9   (c) 10

4. (a) $\frac{4}{5}$ (b) $\frac{1}{4}$ (c) $\frac{3}{5}$

5. (a) $\frac{3}{10}$ (b) $\frac{1}{10}$ (c) $\frac{2}{9}$

6. (a) $\frac{5}{7}$ (b) $\frac{1}{2}$

7. (a) $\frac{1}{6}$ (b) $\frac{3}{10}$

2 Equivalent Fractions (^{US}pp. 70-74 ^{3d}pp. 57-61)

1. (a) 4   (b) 6   (c) 8

    (d) $\frac{10}{15}$, $\frac{12}{18}$, $\frac{14}{21}$

2. (a) 2; 3; $\frac{8}{8}$ (b) 2; 9; $\frac{4}{12}$

3. (a) 3   (b) 6   (c) 2

    (d) 18   (e) 10   (f) 8

4. 4; 34; 3

5. (a) 4   (b) 1   (c) 2

    (d) 3   (e) 4   (f) 6

6. 6; 4; 2; $\frac{1}{2}$

7. (a) $\frac{1}{2}$ (b) $\frac{3}{4}$

(c) $\frac{1}{2}$ (d) $\frac{1}{3}$

(e) $\frac{1}{3}$ (f) $\frac{2}{3}$

(g) $\frac{5}{6}$ (h) $\frac{3}{5}$

8. $\frac{3}{4}$

9. $\frac{7}{10}$

10. (a) $\frac{5}{6}$ (b) $\frac{1}{2}$ (c) $\frac{3}{5}$

11. (a) $\frac{7}{10}$ (b) $\frac{5}{6}$ (c) $\frac{3}{5}$

12. (a) $\frac{1}{2}$, $\frac{5}{8}$, $\frac{3}{4}$ (b) $\frac{3}{10}$, $\frac{2}{5}$, $\frac{3}{5}$

Practice 6B (^{US}p. 75 ^{3d}p. 62)

1. (a) 2   (b) 9   (c) 2, 3

    (d) 2   (e) 2   (f) 2, 3

2. (a) 10   (b) 12   (c) 6, 9

    (d) 2   (e) 4   (f) 6, 10

3. (a) $\frac{7}{10}$ (b) $\frac{5}{6}$ (c) $\frac{10}{12}$

    (d) $\frac{5}{6}$ (e) $\frac{3}{4}$ (f) $\frac{5}{8}$

4. (a) $\frac{1}{7}$, $\frac{3}{7}$, $\frac{5}{7}$ (b) $\frac{1}{10}$, $\frac{1}{5}$, $\frac{1}{2}$

    (c) $\frac{1}{2}$, $\frac{2}{3}$, $\frac{5}{6}$ (d) $\frac{1}{4}$, $\frac{5}{12}$, $\frac{2}{3}$

5. ^{US}Sara ^{3d}Suchen

Review D (^{US}pp. 76-77 ^{3d}pp.63-64)

1. (a) 9210   (b) 4060

2. (a) six thousand, two hundred four

    (b) three thousand, five hundred forty

    (c) five thousand, twenty-eight

3. 3900

4. (a) 4014, 4041, 4104, 4410

    (b) 1112, 2111, 2121, 2211

5. 1000

6. 62 r4

7. 11

8. (a) 20   (b) 30

9. (a) 3   (b) 9   (c) 5

10. (a) $\frac{1}{4}$ (b) $\frac{2}{7}$ (c) $\frac{11}{12}$

    (d) $\frac{3}{6}$ (e) $\frac{3}{8}$ (f) $\frac{2}{5}$

11. (a) 420 cm   (b) 2 m 5 cm
   (c) 2095 m   (d) 1 km 600 m
   (e) 1040 g   (f) 2 kg 450 g
   (g) 3060 ml   (h) 2 ℓ 525 ml
12. 80¢
13. $28.80
14. 675
15. 1 ℓ 250 ml
16. $\frac{5}{9}$
17. $\frac{4}{7}$

Unit 7 - Time

1 Hours and Minutes
(^{US}pp. 78-85 ^{3d}pp. 65-72)

2. (a) 2:05   (b) 4:15
  (c) 12:20   (d) 7:30
  (e) 3:40   (f) 7:45
3. 9:56
4. 60 minutes
5. (a) 27   (b) 5
  (c) 2 h 15 min
6. (a) Jane   (b) ^{US}Amy ^{3d}Aihua
7. 95
8. (a) 120 min (b) 130 min (c) 165 min
  (d) 180 min (e) 185 min (f) 195 min
9. 3 h 20 min
10. (a) 1 h 10 min   (b) 1 h 25 min
   (c) 1 h 40 min   (d) 2 h 5 min
   (e) 2 h 40 min   (f) 3 h 30 min
11. 1 h 5 min
12. 9:00 a.m.
13. 8:30 p.m.
14. (a) 2 h
   (b) 3 h 30 min
   (c) 1 h 15 min
16. (a) 4 h
   (b) 6 h 40 min
   (c) 2 h 50 min
18. (a) 5 h 40 min   (b) 3 h 5 min
   (c) 1 h 15 min   (d) 2 h 35 min
   (e) 3 h 40 min   (f) 5 h 5 min
   (g) 2 h 15 min   (h) 1 h 40 min

Practice 7A (^{US}p. 86 3d p. 73)

1. (a) 3 h 45 min   (b) 1 h 40 min
  (c) 3 h   (d) 1 h 15 min
  (e) 3 h 20 min   (f) 40 min
2. 2:25
3. (a) 7 h 15 min   (b) 1 h 15 min

  (c) 1 h 55 min   (d) 45 min
4. (a) 4 h 30 min   (b) 40 min
5. 11:50 a.m.
6. 12:40 p.m.
7. 8:50 a.m.

2 Other Units of Time
(^{US}pp. 87-88 ^{3d}pp. 74-75)

2. (a) 220 s   (b) 2 min 30 s
3. (a) 12 months   (b) 24 months
  (c) 28 months   (d) 3 years 4 months
4. (a) 7 days
  (b) 21 days
  (c) 25 days
  (d) 4 weeks 2 days

Practice 7B (^{US}p. 89 ^{3d}p. 76)

1. (a) 132 min   (b) 1 h 48 min
  (c) 123   (d) 1 min 34 s
  (e) 21 months   (f) 2 years 6 months
  (g) 19 days   (h) 5 weeks 5 days
2. 1 h 40 min
3. 7 h 30 min
4. 2:20 p.m.
5. 56 min
6. 45 min
7. 5:30 a.m.

Review E (^{US}pp. 90-91 ^{3d}pp. 77-78)

1. (a) 8:55 p.m.
  (b) 1:30 a.m.
2. (a) 4   (b) 8   (c) 8
3. (a) 15   (b) 15
^{US}4. Mr. Lee, 9 months longer
^{3d}4. Mr Lin, 9 months longer
5. 14
6. 6:25 p.m.
7. 6 ℓ
8. $\frac{3}{8}$ m
9. $8.30
10. 68
11. $7.30
12. (a) $48   (b) $6

Unit 8 - Geometry

1 Angles (^{US}pp. 92-93 ^{3d}pp. 79-80)

   a is the smallest, c is the biggest
1. 3 sides, 3 angles
2. 4

2 Right Angles (^{US}pp. 94-95 ^{3d}pp. 81-82)

b, c, d, f
1. (a) 4   (b) 4
2. B   C
3. P - 4 angles, 1 right angle
    Q - 5 angles, 2 right angles
    R - 4 angles, 2 right angles
    S - 5 angles, 3 right angles

Unit 9 - Area and Perimeter

1 Area (^{US}pp. 96-100 ^{3d}pp. 83-87)

6
1. A 6   B 5 C 13   D 6
    E 7   F 10G 10   H 12
    B has the smallest area,
    C has the greatest area
2. 4 cm^2 9 cm^2 16 cm^2
3. (a) 25 cm^2 (b) 100 cm^2
4. 10 cm^2
5. A 5 cm^2 B 8 cm^2 C 5 cm^2
    D 6 cm^2 E 7 cm^2
    F 6 cm^2 G 7 cm^2 H 4 cm^2
6. A 6 m^2 B 4 m^2 C 5 m^2
    A has the greatest area,
    B has the smallest area

2 Perimeter (^{US}pp. 101-104 ^{3d}pp. 88-91)

24
1. Y
3. (a) 6 cm^2
    (b) A - 12 cm   B - 14 cm
4. (a) no   (b) yes
5. (a) Q and S
    (b) R and S
    (c) P and T
6. (a) 24 cm   (b) 32 cm
7. A 25 cm   B 34 m
    C 30 cm   D 39 m

3 Area of a Rectangle (^{US}pp. 105-106 ^{3d}pp.92-93)

A 8 cm^2 B 15 cm^2
C 21 cm^2 D 20 cm^2
1. 20
2. (a) 12 cm^2 (b) 18 cm^2 (c) 24 cm^2
    (d) 27 cm^2 (e) 160 cm^2

Practice 9A (^{US}p. 107 ^{3d}p. 94)

1. (a) a = 25 cm^2, p = 20 cm
    ^{US}(b) a = 170 in.^{2}, p = 54 in.
    ^{3d}(b) a = 170 cm^2, p = 54 cm
    (c) a = 108 cm^2, p = 48 cm
    ^{US}(d) a = 64 ft^2, p = 32 ft
    ^{3d}(d) a = 64 cm^2, p = 32 cm
    (e) a = 162 cm^2, p = 54 cm
2. 150 cm^2
3. 190 m

Review F (^{US}pp. 108-109 ^{3d}pp.95-96)

1. (a) $\frac{1}{2}, \frac{5}{8}, \frac{3}{4}$ (b) $\frac{3}{10}, \frac{1}{2}, \frac{3}{5}$
2. 27 cm
3. (a) 9   (b) 14   (c) 8
4. 2 m 40 cm
5. (a) 900   (b) 2020
6. $32
7. 36 cm^2
8. $\frac{3}{5}$
9. 420 m
10. (a) 2 kg 400 g   (b) 1 kg 500 g
11. (a) B & C   (b) A & B

^{US}Review G (^{US}pp. 110-112)

1. 5280
2. (a) 114 in.
    (b) 70 in.
    (c) 91 in.
3. (a) 6 lb 9 oz   (b) 14 ft 1 in.
    (c) 19 qt   (d) 5 lb 6 oz
    (e) 2 ft 10 in.   (f) 6 gal 3 qt
4. 2 lb 3 oz,   3 lb 8 oz
5. 2 lb 14 oz
6. 2 ft 9 in.
7. 1 c
8. 3 gal 3 qt
9. D
10. 33 in.
11. 12 lb
12. 13 oz
13. 23 lb 15 oz
14. 1 ft 7 in.
15. D, A, C, B
16. Area of square = 36 in.^{2}
    Area of rectangle = 144 ft^2
17. 72 quarts
18. 8 ft
19. 62 lb 10 oz
20. 520 ft

Workbook Answer Key

Exercise 1

1. (a) 92   (b) 83
   (c) 95   (d) 106
2. (a) 91   (b) 57
   (c) 98   (d) 135
   (e) 106   (f) 104
3. (a) 95, 100   (b) 114, 120
4. (a) 92   (b) 70
   (c) 92   (d) 109

Exercise 2

1. (a) 92   (b) 86
   (c) 130   (d) 123
   (e) 145   (f) 140
   (g) 150   (h) 85
2. (a) 60   (b) 100
   (c) 70   (d) 90
   (e) 100   (f) 100
   (g) 90   (h) 100
3. (a) 105   (b) 102
   (c) 141   (d) 166
   (e) 182   (f) 135
   (g) 190   (h) 195
   (i) 197   (j) 198

Exercise 3

1. follow arrows:
   12, 5, 90, 27, 27, 68, 65, 38, 12
2. (a) 66, 62, 62
   (b) 47, 40, 40
   (c) 7, 2, 2
3. (a) 22   (b) 10
   (c) 60   (d) 3
4. (a) 22   (b) 13
   (c) 41   (d) 42

Exercise 4

1. (a) 12, 120 (b) 15, 150 (c) 20, 200
   (d) 35, 350 (e) 24, 2400
2. 16   160   1600
   21   210   2100
   24   240   2400
   40   400   4000
   36   360   3600
   56   560   5600

3. (a) 12, 120 (b) 8, 800
   (c) 400   (d) 120
   (e) 140   (f) 320
   (g) 200   (h) 810
   (i) 180   (j) 140
   (k) 2400   (l) 4800
   (m) 3600   (n) 3000
   (o) 2800   (p) 600
   (q) 1800   (r) 3500

Exercise 5

1. (a) 4, 40   (b) 3, 30   (c) 2, 20
   (d) 3, 300   (e) 4, 400
2. 3   30   300
   4   40   400
   5   50   500
   3   30   300
   4   40   400
   3   30   300
3. (a) 5, 50   (b) 5, 500
   (c) 20   (d) 80
   (e) 90   (f) 50
   (g) 60   (h) 80
   (i) 50   (j) 70
   (k) 900   (l) 800
   (m) 500   (n) 700
   (o) 500   (p) 600
   (q) 900   (r) 400

Exercise 6

1. (a) 47   (b) 15   (c) 26
   (d) 22   (e) 3   (f) 38
2. Answers will vary.
3. (a) 200   (b) 300
   (c) 500   (d) 900
4. (a) 4   (b) 6
   (c) 7   (d) 8
5. (a) 150   (b) 328   (c) 509
6. (a) 2 m 10 cm
   (b) 2 m 75 cm
   (c) 3 m 6 cm
7. (a) shorter than
   (b) equal to
   (c) longer than
8. (a) 10   (b) 35
   (c) 95   (d) 70

Exercise 7

1. (a) 3 m 85 cm
    (b) 4 m 70 cm
    (c) 6 m 10 cm
2. (a) 4 m 20 cm
    (b) 5 m 85 cm
    (c) 7 m 68 cm
    (d) 4 m 26 cm
    (e) 7 m 18 cm
3. (a) 1 m 10 cm
    (b) 2 m 59 cm
    (c) 6 m 39 cm
4. (a) 1 m 89 cm
    (b) 4 m 12 cm
    (c) 3 m 85 cm
    (d) 3 m 86 cm

[US]Exercise 8

1. 950 m → 50 m   860 m → 140 m
    570 m → 430 m   650 m → 350 m
    480 m → 520 m   820 m → 180 m
    210 m → 790 m   670 m → 330 m
2. (a) 20   (b) 110
    (c) 210   (d) 580
    (e) 80   (f) 120
3. (a) 608 km   (b) Malacca, 82 km
4. (a) 23 km   (b) 90 km   (c) 65 km
    (d) 19 km   (e) 6 km
5. (a) 2000   (b) 4000
    (c) 5000   (d) 8000
6. (a) 3   (b) 6
    (c) 7   (d) 9
7. (a) 1145   (b) 3050   (c) 1298
    (d) 2078   (e) 2580
    (f) 1006   (g) 3670
8. (a) 1 km 732 m
    (b) 1 km 305 m
    (c) 2 km 245 m
    (d) 1 km 300 m
    (e) 3 km 260 m
    (f) 3 km 6 m
    (g) 2 km 108 m
9. (a) longer than
    (b) longer than
    (c) shorter than
10. (a) 741 m
    (b) 1 km 865 m or 1865 m
    (c) well, 1 km 124 m or 1124 m
    (d) 1 km 936 m or 1936 m
    (e) 2 km 601 m

[3d]Exercise 8

1. 950 m → 50 m   860 m → 140 m
    570 m → 430 m   650 m → 350 m
    480 m → 520 m   820 m → 180 m
    210 m → 790 m   670 m → 330 m
2. (a) 20   (b) 110   (c) 210
    (d) 580   (e) 80   (f) 120

[3d]Exercise 9

1. (a) 608 km   (b) Malacca, 82 km
2. (a) 23 km   (b) 90 km   (c) 65 km
    (d) 19 km   (e) 6 km
3. (a) 2000   (b) 4000
    (c) 5000   (d) 8000
4. (a) 3   (b) 6
    (c) 7   (d) 9

[3d]Exercise 10

1. (a) 1145   (b) 3050   (c) 1298
    (d) 2078   (e) 2580
    (f) 1006   (g) 3670
2. (a) 1 km 732 m
    (b) 1 km 305 m
    (c) 2 km 245 m
    (d) 1 km 300 m
    (e) 3 km 260 m
    (f) 3 km 6 m
    (g) 2 km 108 m
3. (a) longer than
    (b) longer than
    (c) shorter than
4. (a) 741 m
    (b) 1 km 865 m or 1865 m
    (c) well, 1 km 124 m or 1124 m
    (d) 1 km 936 m or 1936 m
    (e) 2 km 601 m

[US]Exercise 9
[3d]Exercise 11

1. (a) 1 km 850 m
    (b) 3 km 180 m
    (c) 5 km 230 m
2. (a) 6 km 110 m   (b) 7 km 970 m
    (c) 10 km 200 m   (d) 6 km 150 m
    (e) 9 km 200 m   (f) 11 km 100 m
3. (a) 2 km 70 m
    (b) 3 km 940 m
    (c) 5 km 260 m
4. (a) 2 km 650 m   (b) 5 km 920 m
    (c) 3 km 750 m   (d) 6 km 920 m

[US]Exercise 10

1. (a) 29   (b) 10
   (c) 381   (d) 602
2. (a) 5 yd 0 ft   (b) 8 yd 1 ft
   (c) 101 yd 2 ft   (d) 200 yd 0 ft
3. (a) 23   (b) 101   (c) 122
   (d) 34   (e) 81   (f) 108
4. (a) equal to
   (b) shorter than
   (c) longer than
   (d) longer than
   (e) equal to
   (f) shorter than
5. (a) 811 ft or 270 yd 1 ft
   (b) 785 ft or 261 yd 2 ft
   (c) D; 22 ft or 7 yd 1 ft
   (d) 1128 ft

[US]Exercise 11

1. (a) 2 ft 4 in.   (b) 3 ft 7 in.
   (c) 6 ft 7 in.   (d) 4 yd 1 ft
2. (a) 5 yd 1 ft   (b) 9 yd 0 ft
   (c) 21 yd 1 ft   (d) 11 ft 5 in.
   (e) 13 ft 0 in.   (f) 10 ft 4 in.
3. (a) 2 ft 2 in.   (b) 4 ft 9 in.
   (c) 7 ft 11 in.
   (d) 5 yd 0 ft   (e) 1 yd 2 ft
4. (a) 1 yd 2 ft   (b) 1 yd 0 ft
   (c) 1 yd 2 ft   (d) 0 ft 4 in.
   (e) 4 ft 8 in.   (f) 0 ft 10 in.
5. (a) longer than
   (b) longer than
6. (a) 9756 mi
   (b) 2144 mi

Exercise 12

2. (a) 2 kg 500 g   (b) 1 kg 200 g
3. (a) 1 kg 400 g   (b) 2 kg 700 g
   (c) 1 kg 700 g   (d) 3 kg 700 g

[US]Exercise 13

1. (a) 1 kg   (b) 200 g
   (c) 550 g   (d) 330 g
   (e) 250 g   (f) 610 g
   (g) 850 g   (h) 780 g
2. 9 kg 950 g → 9950 g
   9 kg 95 g → 9095 g
   9 kg 905 g → 9905 g
   9 kg 59 g → 9059 g
   9 kg 590 g → 9590 g

3. 1 kg 10 g → 1010 g
   1 kg 100 g → 1100 g
   1 kg 250 g → 1250 g
   1 kg 25 g → 1025 g
   2 kg 25 g → 2025 g
   2 kg 50 g → 2050 g
   3 kg 80 g → 3080 g
   3 kg 8 g → 3008 g
4. (a) 1800   (b) 6020
   (c) 2300   (d) 9002
   (e) 4083   (f) 8015
5. (a) 1 kg 280 g   (b) 4 kg 69 g
   (c) 2 kg 506 g   (d) 5 kg 108 g
   (e) 3 kg 9 g   (f) 6 kg 4 g
6. (a) lighter than   (b) equal to
   (c) lighter than   (d) equal to
7. (a) hen, duck   (b) A, B
8. (a) D   (b) B
   (c) B   (d) D
   (c) 1 kg 700 g   (d) 3 kg 700 g

[3d]Exercise 13

1. (a) 1 kg   (b) 200 g
   (c) 550 g   (d) 330 g
   (e) 250 g   (f) 610 g
   (g) 850 g   (h) 780 g
2. 9 kg 950 g → 9950 g
   9 kg 95 g → 9095 g
   9 kg 905 g → 9905 g
   9 kg 59 g → 9059 g
   9 kg 590 g → 9590 g
3. 1 kg 10 g → 1010 g
   1 kg 100 g → 1100 g
   1 kg 250 g → 1250 g
   1 kg 25 g → 1025 g
   2 kg 25 g → 2025 g
   2 kg 50 g → 2050 g
   3 kg 80 g → 3080 g
   3 kg 8 g → 3008 g

[3d]Exercise 14

1. (a) 1800   (b) 6020
   (c) 2300   (d) 9002
   (e) 4083   (f) 8015
2. (a) 1 kg 280 g   (b) 4 kg 69 g
   (c) 2 kg 506 g   (d) 5 kg 108 g
   (e) 3 kg 9 g   (f) 6 kg 4 g
3. (a) lighter than   (b) equal to
   (c) lighter than   (d) equal to
4. (a) hen, duck   (b) A, B

5. (a) D   (b) B
   (c) B   (d) D

^{US}Exercise 14
^{3d}Exercise 15

1. (a) 1 kg 850 g
   (b) 3 kg 250 g   (c) 4 kg 280 g
2. (a) 3 kg 765 g   (b) 6 kg 250 g
   (c) 6 kg 55 g   (d) 8 kg 9 g
3. (a) 4 kg 90 g
   (b) 4 kg 545 g   (c) 6 kg 635 g
4. (a) 1 kg 156 g   (b) 2 kg 742 g
   (c) 850 g   (d) 6 kg 736 g

^{US}Exercise 15
^{3d}Exercise 16

1. (a) 280 g   (b) 180 g
2. (a) 370 g   (b) 220 g
3. (a) 330 g   (b) 200 g   (c) 100 g
4. (a) 330 g   (b) 120 g, 210 g
   (c) 42 g
5. (a) 5 kg   (b) $1
6. (a) 2 kg   (b) $3

^{US}Exercise 16

1. (a) 3 lb 8 oz
   (b) 6 lb 10 oz
2. (a) 32 oz   (b) 58 oz
   (c) 137 oz
3. (a) 1 lb 2 oz
   (b) 1 lb 6 oz
   (c) 2 lb 0 oz
4. (a) heavier than
   (b) lighter than
   (c) equal to
   (d) heaver than
5. (a) 13 lb 1 oz
   (b) 12 lb 0 oz
   (c) 7 lb 1 oz
6. (a) 2 lb 6 oz (b) 1 lb 14 oz
   (c) 0 lb 15 oz
7. (a) 3 lb   (b) $3
8. 17 lb 1 oz

Review 1

1. odd: 9, 13, 127, 1229
   even: 6, 72, 354, 1350
2. 800, 400, 300, 60, 10
3. (a) 6250   (b) 45,403
   (c) 5000   (d) 2009

4. (a) 8   (b) 45   (c) ^{US}3 ^{3d}65
   (d) 930   (e) 310   (f) ^{US}1 ^{3d}520
   (g) 940   (h) 210   (i) ^{US}8 ^{3d}160
5. 1 km 870 m
6. ^{US}5 lb 1 oz ^{3d}5 kg 610 g
7. 2 kg 304 g
8. $2
9. $109
10. $8.00

Review 2

1. $18
2. 70
3. 9
4. 4 km 800 m
5. ^{US} 7 lb 4 oz ^{3d}4 kg 300 g
6. 769
7. 120
8. 348 g
9. $1700

Exercise 17

1. (c) 1000
2. 5

Exercise 19

1. left side:
   300 ml, 1 ℓ, 400 ml, 800 ml, 700 ml
   right side:
   100 ml, 600 ml, 200 ml, 500 ml, 900 ml
2. (a) 400 ml (b) 700 ml
   (c) 350 ml (d) 150 ml
   (e) 30 ml   (f) 800 ml

Exercise 20

1. 890 → 110   725 → 275
   495 → 505   645 → 355
2. (a) 930 ml (b) 450 ml
   (c) 370 ml (d) 920 ml
3. (a) 140 ml (b) 580 ml
   (c) 250 ml (d) 660 ml

Exercise 21

1. 2 ℓ = 2000 ml
   1 ℓ 120 ml = 1120 ml
   1 ℓ 35 ml = 1035 ml
   1 ℓ 350 ml = 1350 ml
   2 ℓ 500 ml = 2500 ml
   2 ℓ 50 ml = 2050 ml
2. (a) 1100   (b) 1725   (c) 1640

(d) 2855   (e) 2025   (f) 3005
3. (a) 1 ℓ 300 ml   (b) 1 ℓ 450 ml
   (c) 2 ℓ 90 ml   (d) 2 ℓ 105 ml
   (e) 3 ℓ 75 ml   (f) 4 ℓ 5 ml
4. (a) more than   (b) less than
   (c) equal to   (d) less than
   (e) less than

[US]Exercise 22

1. (a) 1 ℓ 750 ml   (b) 3 ℓ 0 ml
   (c) 4 ℓ 150 ml   (d) 5 ℓ 490 ml
2. (a) 3 ℓ 760 ml
   (b) 3 ℓ 890 ml   (c) 5 ℓ 70 ml
   (d) 6 ℓ 45 ml   (e) 8 ℓ 14 ml
3. (a) 3 ℓ 180 ml   (b) 4 ℓ 40 ml
   (c) 4 ℓ 670 ml   (d) 5 ℓ 950 ml
4. (a) 2 ℓ 180 ml
   (b) 1 ℓ 64 ml   (c) 2 ℓ 665 ml
   (d) 760 ml   (e) 5 ℓ 721 ml
5. (a) 1 ℓ 950 ml   (b) 4 ℓ 50 ml
6. (a) 2 ℓ   (b) 10 ℓ
   (c) 1 ℓ 600 ml
7. 2 ℓ 250 ml
8. 9 ℓ 550 ml

[3d]Exercise 22

1. (a) 1 ℓ 750 ml   (b) 3 ℓ 0 ml
   (c) 4 ℓ 150 ml   (d) 5 ℓ 490 ml
2. (a) 3 ℓ 760 ml
   (b) 3 ℓ 890 ml   (c) 5 ℓ 70 ml
   (d) 6 ℓ 45 ml   (e) 8 ℓ 14 ml
3. (a) 3 ℓ 180 ml   (b) 4 ℓ 40 ml
   (c) 4 ℓ 670 ml   (d) 5 ℓ 950 ml
4. (a) 2 ℓ 180 ml
   (b) 1 ℓ 64 ml   (c) 2 ℓ 665 ml
   (d) 760 ml   (e) 5 ℓ 721 ml

[3d]Exercise 23

1. (a) 1 ℓ 950 ml   (b) 4 ℓ 50 ml
2. (a) 2 ℓ   (b) 10 ℓ
   (c) 1 ℓ 600 ml
3. 2 ℓ 250 ml
4. 9 ℓ 550 ml

[US]Exercise 23

1. 3 pt → 6 c   16 c → 1 gal
   2 qt → 4 pt   1 gal 3 qt → 7 qt
   4 pt 1 c → 9 c   5 qt 1 pt → 11 pt
2. (a) 9 pt 0 c   (b) 15 gal 2 qt
3. (a) 1 gal 2 qt   (b) 6 qt 1 pt

4. (a) equal to   (b) more than
   (c) less than   (d) more than
5. (a) 8 gal 3 qt   (b) 22 gal 1 qt

Exercise 24

1. (a) 10   (b) 6:45 a.m.
   (c) 4   (d) 6:30 a.m.
   (e) 18
2. (a) 4   (b) 2   (c) 62
3. (a) 650   (b) 150   (c) Wed.
   (d) Mon.   (e) 2200

Exercise 25

1. (a) 12   (b) Mary, 18
   (c) Weilin, 9
   (d) 2   (e) Weilin
2. (a) $45
   (b) $10
   (c) [US]Ryan [3d]Raju
   (d) [US]Ryan [3d]Raju
   (e) $185
3. (a) 180   (b) 120   (c) Samy
   (d) John   (e) 160

Review 3

1. 66 → 34   53 → 47   38 → 62
   55 → 45   18 → 82   26 → 74
2. $7.80 → $2.20 $8.75 → $1.25
   $6.55 → $3.45 $5.65 → $4.35
   $4.95 → $5.05 $9.30 → $0.70
3. (a) 310   (b) 2 m 85 cm
   (c) 4050 g   (d) 3 kg 50 g
   (e) 2005 m   (f) 2 km 500 m
   (g) 3060 ml   (h) 4 ℓ 5 ml
4. (a) 7 m 45 cm   (b) 3 km 985 m
   (c) 5 kg 170 g   (d) 2 ℓ 960 ml
5. (a) 1 ℓ 400 ml
   (b) 1 ℓ   (c) 200 ml
6. (a) 50   (b) 300
7. 2717
8. 15
9. $28.50

Review 4

1. (a) 3010   (b) 6000   (c) 4015
   (d) 2308   (e) 1968   (f) 2354
2. (a) 406   (b) 848   (c) 2304
   (d) 28   (e) 38   (f) 50 r2

3.   (a) $1.90
     (b) $106.10
     (c) ^{US}$11.95 ^{3d}$21.95
4.   3 cups
5.   10,188
6.   68
7. $6.25
8. $205

Exercise 26

1. $\dfrac{1}{3}, \dfrac{2}{5}, \dfrac{3}{8}, \dfrac{3}{4}, \dfrac{4}{5}, \dfrac{5}{8}$

2.   (a) $\dfrac{2}{3}$ (b) $\dfrac{7}{8}$

    (c) $\dfrac{5}{9}$ (d) $\dfrac{7}{10}$

Exercise 27

1.   (a) 3, 4   (b) 4, 3   (c) $\dfrac{1}{4}$

2.   (a) 4, 6   (b) 6, 4   (c) $\dfrac{2}{6}$

3.   (a) 3, 10   (b) 10, 3   (c) $\dfrac{7}{10}$

4.   (a) $\dfrac{1}{5}$ (b) $\dfrac{4}{9}$

5. $\dfrac{4}{7} \rightarrow \dfrac{3}{7}$ $\dfrac{5}{7} \rightarrow \dfrac{2}{7}$ $\dfrac{7}{8} \rightarrow \dfrac{1}{8}$

    $\dfrac{3}{8} \rightarrow \dfrac{5}{8}$ $\dfrac{9}{10} \rightarrow \dfrac{1}{10}$ $\dfrac{7}{10} \rightarrow \dfrac{3}{10}$

Exercise 28

1.   (a) $\dfrac{2}{3}$ (b) $\dfrac{3}{4}$ (c) $\dfrac{3}{5}$

    (d) $\dfrac{4}{6}$ (e) $\dfrac{5}{8}$ (f) $\dfrac{5}{9}$

2.   (a) 4, 4, 2   (b)   5, 5, 4
    (c) 6, 6, 3   (d)   8, 8, 7
    (e) 10, 10, 6   (f)   12, 12, 9

Exercise 29

1.   (a) $\dfrac{1}{3}$ (b) $\dfrac{1}{6}$

    (c) $\dfrac{3}{4}$ (d) $\dfrac{2}{3}$

2.   (a) $\dfrac{1}{6}$ (b) $\dfrac{1}{5}$

    (c) $\dfrac{5}{8}$ (d) $\dfrac{3}{10}$

3.   (a) $\dfrac{1}{7}$ (b) $\dfrac{1}{8}$

    (c) $\dfrac{6}{7}$ (d) $\dfrac{7}{8}$

4.   (a) $\dfrac{1}{5}$ (b) $\dfrac{1}{10}$

    (c) $\dfrac{3}{7}$ (d) $\dfrac{5}{12}$

5.   (a) $\dfrac{1}{10}, \dfrac{1}{7}, \dfrac{1}{6}$

    (b) $\dfrac{3}{10}, \dfrac{3}{8}, \dfrac{3}{4}$

    (c) $\dfrac{1}{9}, \dfrac{1}{5}, 1$

6.   (a) $\dfrac{1}{3}, \dfrac{1}{4}, \dfrac{1}{12}$

    (b) $\dfrac{5}{7}, \dfrac{5}{9}, \dfrac{5}{12}$

    (c) $\dfrac{1}{8}, \dfrac{1}{10}, 0$

Exercise 30

1.   (a) $\dfrac{4}{6}, \dfrac{5}{6}$ (b) $\dfrac{5}{8}, \dfrac{6}{8}$

    (c) $\dfrac{8}{12}, \dfrac{10}{12}, 1$ (d) $\dfrac{6}{9}, \dfrac{5}{9}, \dfrac{4}{9}$

    (e) $\dfrac{6}{10}, \dfrac{5}{10}, \dfrac{4}{10}$

2.   (a) $\dfrac{5}{8}$ (b) $\dfrac{2}{6}$

    (c) $\dfrac{4}{5}$ (d) $\dfrac{7}{10}$

3.   (a) $\dfrac{4}{5}$ (b) $\dfrac{6}{7}$

    (c) $\dfrac{7}{10}$ (d) $\dfrac{5}{6}$

4.   (a) $\dfrac{1}{3}$ (b) $\dfrac{1}{5}$

    (c) $\dfrac{4}{10}$ (d) $\dfrac{5}{12}$

5.   (a) $\dfrac{4}{5}$ (b) $\dfrac{6}{7}$

    (c) $\dfrac{8}{9}$ (d) $\dfrac{10}{12}$

6.   (a) $\dfrac{1}{4}$ (b) $\dfrac{2}{6}$

    (c) $\dfrac{4}{10}$ (d) $\dfrac{2}{11}$

7.   (a) $\dfrac{3}{10}, \dfrac{5}{10}, \dfrac{8}{10}$ (b) $\dfrac{3}{12}, \dfrac{5}{12}, 1$

Exercise 31

1. $\frac{5}{6} \rightarrow \frac{10}{12}$ $\frac{2}{3} \rightarrow \frac{6}{9}$

   $\frac{5}{10} \rightarrow \frac{1}{2}$ $\frac{3}{5} \rightarrow \frac{6}{10}$

2. (a) 2   (b) 3   (c) 5
   (d) 2   (e) 4   (f) 10
   (g) 2   (h) 3   (i) 6
   (j) 2   (k) 4   (l) 8

Exercise 32

1. (a) 6; 3   (b) 6; 12   (c) 3; 6

2. (a) $\frac{8}{10}$ (b) $\frac{4}{12}$

3. $\frac{1}{2}, \frac{2}{4}$ $\frac{4}{5}, \frac{8}{10}$ $\frac{1}{4}, \frac{2}{8}$

   $\frac{6}{10}, \frac{3}{5}$ $\frac{2}{6}, \frac{1}{3}$

   $\frac{1}{2}, \frac{5}{10}$ $\frac{2}{6}, \frac{3}{9}$

Exercise 33

1. (a) $\frac{4}{5}$ (b) $\frac{5}{6}$

   (c) $\frac{3}{4}$ (d) $\frac{8}{10}$

   (e) $\frac{1}{2}$ (f) $\frac{2}{3}$

   (g) $\frac{6}{12}$ (h) $\frac{2}{3}$

2. (a) $\frac{4}{6}$ (b) $\frac{8}{10}$ (c) $\frac{2}{5}$

   (d) $\frac{6}{6}$ (e) $\frac{3}{4}$ (f) $\frac{2}{12}$

   (g) $\frac{3}{4}$ (h) $\frac{5}{10}$

Exercise 34

1. (a) $\frac{2}{3}$ (b) $\frac{3}{4}$

2. (a) $\frac{1}{2}$ (b) $\frac{2}{3}$ (c) $\frac{1}{3}$

3. Lucky

4. (1) $\frac{2}{3}$ (2) $\frac{1}{3}$ (3) $\frac{1}{5}$

   (4) $\frac{1}{4}$ (5) $\frac{1}{2}$ (6) $\frac{4}{5}$

   (7) $\frac{3}{4}$ (8) $\frac{5}{6}$ (9) $\frac{1}{6}$

   WATER POLO

Exercise 35

1. (a) $\frac{7}{8}$ (b) $\frac{4}{5}$

   (c) $\frac{2}{3}$ (d) $\frac{2}{3}$

   (e) $\frac{4}{5}$ (f) $\frac{11}{12}$

   (g) $\frac{2}{3}$ (h) $\frac{1}{2}$

2. (a) $\frac{2}{5}, \frac{1}{2}, \frac{5}{6}$

   (b) $\frac{1}{2}, \frac{5}{8}, \frac{3}{4}$

   (c) $\frac{7}{12}, \frac{2}{3}, \frac{5}{6}$

   (d) $\frac{7}{12}, \frac{2}{3}, \frac{3}{4}$

Review 5

1. (a) 60   (b) 300
   (c) 70   (d) 500
2. (a) x   (b) −   (c) ÷
   (d) +   (e) −
3. $405
4. 58 kg
5. 396
6. 680
7. 800 m
8. $13
9. 68
10. 4 kg 800 g
11. US3 ft 8 in.   3d1 m 32 cm
12. 80, 160

Review 6

1. (a) 185   (b) 53   (c) 6700
   (d) 2972   (e) 3654   (f) 2304
3. (a) $\frac{1}{4}$ (b) $\frac{3}{8}$ (c) $\frac{2}{3}$

   (d) $\frac{4}{6}$ (e) $\frac{3}{4}$ (f) $\frac{3}{8}$

5. $255
6. 12
7. US7 oz   3d550 g
8. 1 kg 400 g
9. (a) $20   (b) $2

Exercise 36

1. 7:17   8:03
    2:41   4:36
    4:02   8:14
    11:52   12:21
2. 12:00; noon
    4:42; 18 minutes to 5
    9:10; 10 minutes past 9
    2:45; 15 minutes to 3
    4:55; 5 minutes to 5
    11:05; 5 minutes past 11
    1:27; 27 minutes past 1
    7:25; 25 minutes past 7
    10:36; 24 minutes to 11
    8:53; 7 minutes to 9

Exercise 37

1. (a) 25
    (b) 30, 6:05
    (c) 6:10, 2, 8:10
    (d) 7:25, 3, 10:25
2. (a) 1 h 15 min
    (b) 2:20, 3 h 50, 6:10
    (c) 7:40, 8 h , 3:40
    (d) 8:50, 4 h 25 min, 1:15

Exercise 38

1. 90 min → 1 h 30 min
    120 min → 2 h
    110 min → 1 h 50 min
    130 min → 2 h 10 min
    95 min → 1 h 35 min
    135 min → 2 h 15 min
    210 min → 3 h 30 min
2. (a) 105   (b) 125
    (c) 1 h 25 min   (d) 2 h 30 min
3. (a) 65   (b) 90
    (c) 145   (d) 190
4. (a) 1 h 15 min   (b) 1 h 40 min
    (c) 2 h 20 min   (d) 3 h 45 min

Exercise 39

1. 9:15 p.m.
2. 1 h 20 min
3. 7:10 p.m.
4. 1 h 20 min
5. 8:20 a.m.
6. 25 min

Exercise 40

1. (a) 1 h 55 min   (b) 2 h 25 min
    (c) 3 h 20 min   (d) 3 h 10 min
2. (a) 4 h 10 min   (b) 3 h 10 min
    (c) 4 h 10 min   (d) 4 h 15 min
    (e) 5 h 10 min   (f) 6 h 10 min
3. (a) 1 h 35 min   (b) 2 h 25 min
    (c) 1 h 15 min   (d) 2 h 55 min
4. (a) 1 h 20 min   (b) 1 h 5 min
    (c) 1 h 15 min   (d) 1 h 30 min
    (e) 1 h 45 min   (f) 2 h 55 min

Exercise 41

2. (a) ^{US}Emily ^{3d}Devi
    (b) ^{US}Taylor ^{3d}Sulin
    (c) 4
3. (a) 20   (b) 26
    (c) 45   (d) 34

Exercise 42

1. 60 s, 65 s, 105 s, 120 s,
    145 s, 180 s, 215 s
2. (a) 100 s   (b) 130 s
    (c) 1 min 40 s   (d) 2 min 30 s
3. (a) 85 s   (b) 165 s
    (c) 170 s   (d) 210 s
4. (a) 1 min 30 s   (b) 1 min 55 s
    (c) 2 min 5 s   (d) 3 min 20 s
5. (a) 90 s   (b) 115 s
    (c) 125 s   (d) 150 s
    (e) 185 s   (f) 220 s
    (g) 1 min 20 s   (h) 1 min 25 s
    (i) 1 min 35 s   (j) 1 m 50 s
    (k) 2 m 20 s   (l) 2 m 45 s

Exercise 43

1. 13, 18, 24, 20, 30, 36, 26
2. (a) 17 months
    (b) 2 years 4 months
3. (a) 15 months
    (b) 29 months
    (c) 35 months
    (d) 46 months
4. (a) 1 year 3 months
    (b) 2 years 1 month
    (c) 2 years 8 months
    (d) 3 years 4 months

Exercise 44

1. 7, 10, 14, 13, 16, 20, 22
2. (a) 17 days
   (b) 5 weeks 5 days
3. (a) 12 days
   (b) 18 days
   (c) 24 days
   (d) 30 days
4. (a) 1 week 5 days
   (b) 3 weeks 4 days
   (c) 4 weeks 2 days
   (d) 4 weeks 4 days

Review 7

1. (a) $\frac{7}{10}$ (b) $\frac{5}{6}$
   (c) $\frac{3}{4}$ (d) $\frac{1}{2}$
2. (a) 10:25 a.m.
   (b) 30
3. (a) 4   (b) 30
   (c) 10   (d) 10
4. (a) m   (b) ml   (c) g
   (d) ℓ (e) km
5. (a) 280
   (b) 144
6. $13

Exercise 45

1. A. 4,4   B. 5,5   C. 3,3
   D. 4,4   E. 6,6   F. 5,5

Exercise 46

1. (a) smaller (b) equal (c) bigger
   (d) bigger (e) equal
3. A. 4,4,2   B. 4,4,2   C. 4,4,4
   D. 4,4,2   E. 4,4,2   F. 5,5,3
   G. 3,3,1   H. 4,4,4   I. 4,4,2

Exercise 47

1. A. 9   B. 10   C. 9
   D. 12   E. 11   F. 7
2. A. 9 B. 8   C. 9
   D. 6   E. 9   F. 10

Exercise 48

1. A. 11   B. 11   C. 10
   D. 13   A & B, D, C
2. A. 9 cm^2 B. 5 cm^2
   C. 7 cm^2 D. 8 cm^2

Exercise 49

1. (a) 8 cm^2 (b) 12 cm^2 (c) 5 cm^2
   (d) 6 cm^2 (e) 9 cm^2 (f) 8 cm^2

Exercise 50

1. (a) 14 cm   (b) 16 cm
   (c) 12 cm   (d) 14 cm
   (e) 9 cm   (f) 11 cm
2. (a) A   B   C   D   E   F
       10   13   10   9   8   13
       14   16   16   12   18   16
   (b) A & C   (c) B & C or C & F
   (d) B & F
3. (a) 28 cm   (b) 36 cm
   (c) 34 m   (d) 37 m

Exercise 51

1. A. 4, 2, 8 cm^2
   B. 6, 2, 12 cm^2
   C. 7, 3, 21 cm^2
   D. 5, 3, 15 cm^2
   E. 4, 3, 12 cm^2
2. A. 5, 2, 10 cm^2
   B. 4, 3, 12 cm^2
   C. 6, 4, 24 cm^2
   D. 3, 7, 21 cm^2
   E. 8, 1, 8 cm^2

Exercise 52

1. (a) 12 cm^2 (b) 24 cm^2
   (c) 35 m^2 (d) 54 cm^2
   (e) 40 m^2 (f) 120 cm^2
2. (a) A. 14 m^2, 18 cm
       B. 16 m^2, 16 m
       C. 16 cm^2, 20 m
       D. 20 m^2, 18 m
       E. 12 m^2, 14 m
   (b) E   (c) C
   (d) B & C   (e) A & D

Review 8

1. (a) 32, 40, 48
   (b) 63, 54, 45
   (c) 175, 195, 215
   (d) 1934, 1734, 1534
2. (a) 45   (b) 20   (c) 240
3. (a) 3 h 50 min   (b) 11:35 a.m.
4. (a) 11 cm^2, 16 cm
   (b) 7 m^2, 14 m
5. (a) 35 cm   (b) 36 m

Teacher's Guide 3B: Workbook Answer Key

Review 9

1. (a) 5000   (b) 50
2. (a) 6   (b) 5   (c) 5
3. (a) $\frac{4}{5}$ (b) $\frac{3}{4}$ (c) $\frac{1}{2}$
4. (a) $\frac{2}{6}, \frac{3}{6}, \frac{5}{6}$
   (b) $\frac{4}{9}, \frac{2}{3}, \frac{7}{9}$
   (c) $\frac{3}{8}, \frac{1}{2}, \frac{3}{4}$
5. (a) 30 (5 x 6)
   (b) 10 (40 ÷ 4)
6. (a) 15 m^2
   (b) 16 m^2

7. 1 ℓ 500 ml
8. b
9. 850 m
10. $3.60
11. 6:50 a.m.
12. 70
US13. (a) 3 lb 3 oz
   (b) 16 pt 1 c
   (c) 4 ft 6 in.
US14. $1.65
US15. $10.75
US16. 2 pt